Stress-free flying

Stress-free flying

Robert Bor, Jeannette Josse and Stephen Palmer

Quay Books

Mark Allen
Publishing Ltd

Quay Books Division, Mark Allen Publishing Limited
Jesses Farm, Snow Hill, Dinton, Nr Salisbury, Wilts, SP3 5HN

©Mark Allen Publishing Ltd 2000
ISBN 1 85642 167 8

British Library Cataloguing-in-Publication data
A catalogue record for this book is available from the British
Library

Printed in the UK by The Cromwell Press, Trowbridge, Wiltshire, UK

Contents

About the authors   vii

Foreword by Dr Jane Zuckerman   ix

Introduction   xi

1   Conquering negative travel beliefs and attitudes   1

2   Understanding fears, anxieties and phobias about flying   15

3   Conquering fears and anxieties about flying: a self-help tool kit   33

4   How to survive air terminals   55

5   Coping with jet lag   62

6   The effect of air travel on relationships   74

7   Flying with children   97

8   Understanding passenger behaviour   115

References   131

Index   133

About the authors

Robert Bor is a Professor of Psychology at London Guildhall University and is a Chartered Clinical, Counselling and Health Psychologist and Psychotherapist. He is also a pilot. He works in a travel health clinic and has a special interest in treating people who have a fear of flying. He has published numerous books and articles and is frequently interviewed by the media.

Jeannette Josse qualified in medicine and is a psychiatrist and psychotherapist practising in Cambridge and London. As an experienced traveller she combines her enthusiasm for photography with her interest in people in far-off places. She writes academic and general articles on relationship and health matters.

Stephen Palmer is a Counselling and Health Psychologist, and Honorary Visiting Professor of Psychology at City University. He is also Director of the Centre for Stress Management, London and is a well-known stress expert who is frequently interviewed by the media. He looks forward to watching films on long haul flights.

Foreword

Travel has become an ever increasing fascination with more than 600 million international trips being made annually throughout the world. In the United Kingdom alone, 46 million overseas visits were made by UK residents in 1997. According to the World Tourist Organization, travel to international destinations is projected to increase by 80% from 1995 to 2010.

People of all ages travel for various reasons, from business trips to trekking; the ease and speed of air travel making most destinations accessible. However, stress and anxiety are two features common to all journeys.

It is refreshing to find a practical book which addresses itself solely to the psychological aspects of travel. Its comprehensive review of different situations in which anxiety, fear and phobias occur, and how to manage such situations, makes this book essential reading as well as a necessary companion during travel. Fear of flying is a common phobia for which more and more people express genuine concern and require professional guidance.

Situations associated with stress and travel have become more recognised and, to some degree, reflect present society and the pace of life. Air rage, consumption of alcohol and drugs all contribute and often exacerbate stressful situations.

This book provides practical guidance for all travellers as well as those who provide travel health advice.

Dr Jane Zuckerman
Head of the Academic Unit of Travel Medicine
Royal Free & University College Medical School, London
1999

Introduction

Air travel has never been so accessible. The dream of flight is a reality for millions of people each year all over the world. A billion people will soon make at least one plane trip per year. If you have bought this book, you may be planning such a trip or already be on your way. You might be experiencing a range of emotions: anticipation, excitement, mild fear or even worry and at the same time be caught up in organising and making the necessary practical arrangements to achieve your goal of a stress-free trip. Unfortunately, the dream of flight, nurtured by Leonardo da Vinci, the Wright Brothers and others, is sometimes tarnished by stress. Approximately twenty years ago, air travel was exciting. It attracted a small number of elite and wealthy passengers and enabled people to travel at greater speeds than ever before. Passengers were pampered and obedient. The advent of large commercial airliners in an industry of mass air transportation and cheap, accessible flights has changed all of this. Airline advertisements raise expectations among air travellers because the product they promote is glamorous. Disappointment sets in when our expectations are not met, and high levels of stress are one outcome of this.

This book can help you to cope better with the stress of modern air travel. We, the authors, all trained in psychology, have experienced and observed at first hand what happens when people travel. We are aware of how air travel disrupts our relationships, sense of time, behaviour, bodily functions and systems, and dispels our fantasies of pleasure in flying. We have treated people who have fears about air travel, whether it is mild apprehension or an incapacitating phobia. Stress and fear associated with air travel can cause strife to business and personal relationships. Travel arrangements may be put off and excuses made. This book will help you, however, to recognise the cause of your travel-related stress and suggest practical ways of overcoming it.

Stress may begin long before setting out for the airport. Making travel arrangements, preparing to leave home and saying 'goodbye' to family, friends or colleagues can increase stress and distress. Once at the airport, crowds, noise, communication difficulties due to language problems, inadequate sign-posting and long walks to the departure gate can test the resilience of even the healthiest travellers. The burdens of airport turmoil are all the greater for the older person, very young and those with any form of disability. Those with any visual impairment may find it stressful to be presented with only visual data about aircraft arrivals and departures.

The mixture of crowds, noise, inconsiderate behaviour, apprehension about travel, ambiguous or incomprehensible information, may make you, the traveller, feel physically and psychologically vulnerable and stressed. Of course, this may be accentuated if you are tired, overly stressed or if you tend to become aggressive, anxious or irritable in response to these challenges. There may also be a tendency to over-react to travel problems and situations if you have an expectation that the trip is a 'get away from it all' holiday designed to alleviate stress.

Most passengers have expectations about travel, and these may be built around punctuality, quality of service, or amenities available at airports or on board aircraft. There will be times when these expectations are not met, due to delays or poor levels of service; these may be unpredictable but no less annoying as a result. Passengers react differently to stress. Some resort to alcohol consumption to relieve boredom, anxiety or irritation, while others become militant about what they believe to be their 'rights' and may become insistent or hostile towards ground staff or cabin crew. Others resort to taking medication to reduce anxiety or induce sleep. Each of these coping strategies may, however, further aggravate the situation and increase stress.

One of the unique features of this book is its approach to dealing with the specific stresses of flying. So often travellers, quite rightly, blame the airlines for some of the problems that arise on their journey. However, this does not reduce their levels of stress when the inevitable goes wrong. Believe it or not, airlines are fallible too. This book will help you to challenge your stress-inducing beliefs and attitudes that cause you so much stress. Instead of upsetting yourself about how things 'should be' we will examine other thinking styles that will help you to deal with the adversity that arises on some journeys, and how to resolve problems without making huge mountains out of molehills.

Each chapter in this book addresses different problems for the air traveller including: managing your expectations and beliefs about travel, coping with a fear of flying, how to relax, overcoming jet lag, how travel disrupts relationships and what to do about this, travelling with children, the special needs of the elderly and understanding how air travel affects passengers' behaviour. Our aim has been to offer an understanding of these issues as well as to give practical advice and self-help methods of coping with these problems and situations.

Air travel provides a wonderful opportunity in which to view oneself differently: you are in an unfamiliar setting, surrounded by strangers, overcoming a natural law (gravity) and from the vantage point of 35,000 feet you can look down on everyday life and gain new perspectives. Everyone experiences some apprehension and exhilaration at this. Air travel is not merely a convenient and efficient form of transport; it is an experience that can have a powerful emotional effect. In this book we hope that you will find many practical hints and advice on how to cope with the stress of travel, and gain a clearer understanding of your emotions when travelling by air.

1
Conquering negative travel beliefs and attitudes

In this chapter we will be considering the expectations, beliefs, attitudes and ideas that travellers and holidaymakers have that lead to unnecessary stress and grief, not only for themselves but for others too.

Think back to the last time you went on holiday, or perhaps you were just travelling abroad on a business trip. At any point did you become stressed, fed up or really angry? Imagine the situation is happening again. What thoughts or ideas were going through your mind at the time? For example,

- if you were stressed or anxious did you perceive the situation as 'threatening' or 'awful'
- if you were fed up, perhaps you were telling yourself that 'life's unfair' or 'things should be better than they are at present'
- if you were feeling angry perhaps you demanded that 'the weather should be excellent' or 'I must be treated in a civil manner'.

Often, it is these ideas that largely contribute to how you feel about a situation and not the situation itself. This was recognised almost two thousand years ago by first century philosophers such as Epictetus who observed,

> *People are disturbed not by things but by the views which they take of them.*

Later, in the second century, Marcus Aurelius also reflected on this issue in his *Meditations,*

> *Put from you the belief that "I have been wronged", and with it will go the feeling. Reject your sense of injury, and the injury itself disappears.*

He went on to describe how this occurs,

> *For you, badness comes not from the mind of another; nor yet from any of the phases and changes of your own bodily frame. Then whence? From that part of yourself which acts as your assessor of what is bad.*

So what was his solution to the problem? He continued,

> *Refuse its assessment, and all is well... Everything is but what your opinion makes it; and that opinion lies with yourself. Renounce it when you will, and at once you have rounded the foreland and all is calm; a tranquil sea, a tideless haven.*

In other words, mentally re-appraise the situation and you will feel less stressed and perhaps even relaxed. And this is without doing relaxation exercises or meditation. This may sound remarkable but has been known for centuries. Shakespeare even noted in *Hamlet* (II.ii 259–61),

> *Why, then 'tis none to you; for there is nothing good or bad but thinking makes it so.*

Common unhelpful negative beliefs and attitudes can lead to stress.

Let us examine a number of demands or expectations travellers or holidaymakers may have. Dr. Stephen Palmer at the Centre for Stress Management in London developed a simple Negative Travel Beliefs Questionnaire (NTBQ, 1999) to help travellers analyse their own negative beliefs. Do you recognise any of the following? Circle the strength of your belief as follows: 'S' represents strongly, 'M' represents moderately and 'W' represents weakly. Include in Question 24 any additional beliefs that you hold that cause you further stress.

Negative travel beliefs questionnaire (NTBQ)

1.	S	M	W	The journey should go smoothly
2.	S	M	W	The weather should be excellent
3.	S	M	W	The food must be good
4.	S	M	W	The accommodation should be of a very high standard
5.	S	M	W	New places must be exciting
6.	S	M	W	New people must be exciting
7.	S	M	W	The entertainment must be good
8.	S	M	W	I/We must enjoy ourselves
9.	S	M	W	I/We must not get bored
10.	S	M	W	I/We must not encounter problems
11.	S	M	W	I/We must have the solitude I/we deserve
12.	S	M	W	I/We must have the nightlife I/we deserve
13.	S	M	W	I/We must escape from responsibilities and demands
14.	S	M	W	I/We should be able to let our hair down
15.	S	M	W	I/We must be treated fairly
16.	S	M	W	I/We should be treated as special
17.	S	M	W	I/We must be in control of all situations
18.	S	M	W	We should get on well together as friends/family
19.	S	M	W	If things go badly then it would be awful

20.	S	M	W	If things go badly I could not stand it
21.	S	M	W	Things never go well on my trips and holidays
22.	S	M	W	I am indispensible at work therefore I should not have time off
23.	S	M	W	If things go wrong then those responsible are 'stupid', 'useless', 'idiots', or 'failures'
24.	S	M	W	Additional beliefs

Surprisingly, if you hold onto just one of these beliefs strongly, then when an event occurs that does not live up to its expectations you are likely to suffer from stress. The more beliefs you hold strongly or even moderately, the more stress you are likely to encounter on a simple journey or holiday trip. If you scored more than ten strongly, then it is highly likely that **you** make most long distant journeys or holidays a nightmare. Even if you hold any of the above beliefs only moderately, under extremes of pressure you are likely to become quite stressed. Let us look at a case study.

Case study

Erik had an important presentation to make to the Board of Directors in New York. He had meticulously prepared for his presentation and was in good spirits before leaving home. However, although he arrived at the airport in good time, his flight from London Heathrow was delayed. As he became impatient he muttered, 'This is awful. This should not be happening to me'. As he mulled over his thoughts he gradually became more anxious about the possibility of arriving late. 'Oh my God,' he thought, 'This could affect my future promotion'. This negative fortune-telling made him feel very stressed. He then went up to the airline enquiries desk and gave them a piece of his mind. 'Your airline is really useless. This is the last time I'm flying with you. You never get it right!' At this point he was feeling extremely angry as he voiced his thoughts. Although the staff told him that the delay would not be for long, he was very wound up and found it difficult to relax. To unwind, he went to a bar and had a drink or two. Unfortunately, once he had started it was too tempting not to have another couple of drinks on the plane too. Consequently, when he finally arrived at JFK airport he was feeling rather rough and not looking forward to giving the presentation.

In this case example, we can examine the precise negative beliefs that largely contributed to Erik's stress levels. These include:

'This is awful.'

'This should not be happening to me.'

'Oh my God. This could affect my future promotion.'

These negative thoughts made Erik feel very anxious. Initially, he started to 'awfulise' and think that things were as bad as they could ever get. When people see the worst they exaggerate how bad things really are by using words similar to 'awful' to describe a situation, such as 'horrendous', 'terrible', 'horrible', 'it's a catastrophe', 'the end of the world', or they blaspheme, for example, 'Oh God', or 'Oh Christ'. Erik then thought it 'should not' be happening, even though it was; a direct denial of reality. Then to make matters worse, he started making negative predictions about the future as if he had superhuman powers of clairvoyance.

'This could affect my future promotion.'

'Your airline is really useless.'

'This is the last time I'm flying with you.'

'You never get it right.'

When he started to label the airline as 'really useless' it was a certain way of becoming angry. So often when people label, they start overgeneralising and instead of just rating one error or deficit they globally label every aspect of the person, organisation or thing as 'totally useless', 'bad', 'a failure', or 'worthless' which, of course, is rarely the case.

In this case, Erik's labelling subsequently led to 'all-or-nothing' thinking in which he decided not to fly with them again and condemned them for 'never' getting it right. These extreme thinking styles seldom help to resolve difficult situations. By this time he had wound himself up so much that he needed a few drinks to help relax before and during the flight. He had forgotten his goal which was to give a good presentation and was the worse for wear on his arrival in New York.

It is worth noting that there have been many travellers in similar situations who did not become stressed at all and used the extra time available to prepare thoroughly their presentations or conference papers. We will return to this case study later and consider what Erik could have done instead.

One more case study will highlight the stresses caused by the expectations holidaymakers sometimes hold.

Case study

Jayne and Sean decided to take a week's break in China. They had been very busy for some months with their respective work and this was impacting upon their relationship. They both thought it was time to 'get to know each other again'. Although the journey to Beijing went reasonably well, on arrival things took a turn for the worse.

Jayne went to the toilet and by the time she had returned the other passengers had disappeared. It was not clear where Sean and she should go and talking to the airport staff proved rather difficult. Sean became annoyed and told Jayne what he thought of the staff, 'Bloody idiots. They should employ staff that can speak English!' He was also feeling quite tired as he had not managed to get any sleep on the flight. 'Oh come on Sean. Please don't cause a scene. Let's just chill out and enjoy ourselves,' Jayne retorted. Sean was not going to have any of this and replied in an angry tone, 'Don't you lecture me. They should be prepared to help tourists'. Unfortunately, Jayne took this comment rather personally and she became tearful. The holiday was off to a bad start and it was not going as well as 'it should do'. In her mind this was more evidence that she was a 'failure' and their relationship was over.

Again, we can examine the negative beliefs that exacerbated a difficult situation. These are:

> 'Bloody idiots.'

> 'They should employ staff who can speak English.'

Sean became angry when he labelled the staff as 'bloody idiots'. He then demanded that 'they should employ staff that can speak English'. In fact, they could speak English but not the fluent English that he expected. As Jayne so desperately wanted them both to enjoy themselves her response to Sean was like a red rag to a bull. He criticised her for lecturing him and she became upset when she realised that the holiday was not going as well as 'it should do'. She then labelled herself as a 'failure' which is almost guaranteed to make a person feel depressed and tearful.

Challenging unhelpful negative travel beliefs and attitudes

What do psychologists mean by 'unhelpful' or 'negative' beliefs and attitudes? These beliefs have a number of common themes. They are usually:

- illogical, especially dogmatic and demanding (eg. must, should, ought and got to)
- empirically inconsistent with reality (in other words, deny reality and facts)
- obstructive, preventing travellers and holidaymakers from achieving their goals, cause problems, are task-interfering and unconstructive.

This leads us to the next question. What are helpful or realistic beliefs or attitudes? They are usually:

- logical, especially non-absolutist and preferential (eg. wishes, wants, desires and preferences)
- empirically consistent with reality; that is, based on facts
- pragmatic, problem-solving, goal and task-focused and constructive.

Now go back to the NTBQ. If you have not done so already, spend a few minutes completing the questionnaire. It may be helpful to think back to the last time you encountered difficulties on your last trip or holiday. This may help to remind you of one or more of these beliefs. In fact, you may remember additional unhelpful beliefs or attitudes which can be added to the bottom of the NTBQ (question no. 24).

Now, pick a negative belief or attitude that seems to cause

you stress when triggered by an event. You can return to this in a few minutes once we have shown you how to deal with these beliefs.

Let us look at some of Erik's stress-inducing ideas again. It is best to tackle each belief one at a time. There are a number of challenging questions we can ask to help the process.

(a) Negative belief: 'This is awful'

Question:	Is this belief logical? Although the situation may be bad, can we logically conclude that the situation is 'awful'? (A logical challenge.)
Answer:	Probably not.
Question:	Is this belief empirically consistent with reality? In other words, is it realistic? (An empirical challenge.)
Answer:	There's plenty of evidence that the situation is a life hassle, but it really is not a life horror. I'm probably making a mountain out of a molehill.
Question:	Where is holding on to this belief getting me? (A pragmatic challenge.)
Answer:	I'm beginning to feel very anxious that I might arrive late. I am unable to think clearly. I'm beginning to feel very tense and uptight. I might need a drink of alcohol to help me feel better. I'm not being goal or task-focused and certainly not in a problem-solving frame of mind.

(b) Negative belief: 'This should not be happening to me'

Question:	Does it logically follow that just because I would prefer these things not to happen, therefore they should not happen?

Answer: Perhaps I'm not being logical.

Question: Is my belief realistic? What law of the universe says that something 'should not happen'?

Answer: Even though I'm saying that it 'should not be happening' the reality is that it **is** happening. Therefore, I'm denying reality. If anything, it '**should**' be happening as it is happening. Clearly I would prefer it not to happen. That is realistic.

Question: Where is holding onto this belief getting me?

Answer: I'm becoming anxious, tense and wound up. In fact, I am beginning to feel angry too.

(c) Negative belief: 'Your airline is really useless'

Question: Does it logically follow that when the airline has one delay then it becomes 'useless'?

Answer: No. It may have a number of flaws but these don't make it 'useless'. In fact, how many flaws would it take to make anything useless — probably countless flaws. At any rate, both passengers and airline staff are inconvenienced by delays. These are usually beyond the direct control of the airline (eg. weather, technical problems) and no-one would wish to see safety compromised.

Question: Where is the evidence that the airline is 'useless'?

Answer: It may act in a 'useless manner' occasionally but this does not make it totally useless. If it was useless then it would not stay in business for very long. In fact, their planes would hardly ever leave the ground and, if they did, they would probably crash.

Question: Where is holding onto this belief getting me?

Answer: Nowhere. No, that is incorrect. It is getting me somewhere. I am becoming very angry; not only upsetting myself but being unnecessarily difficult to the staff who can't help what has happened. I'm getting so wound up that I am becoming tense and need a drink or two (or more) to help me unwind. Instead of spending the spare time preparing for my important presentation, I am getting angry at the staff and the airline. In fact, after five drinks I won't be up to preparing for my presentation and may arrive wound up, physically and mentally tired and exhausted. This won't look professional at all. It will be me that looks 'useless' in front of the Board of Directors and not the airline. This is really not being goal or task-focused and I am not in a problem-solving frame of mind either.

We have just illustrated a number of logical, empirical and pragmatic questions that Erik could have used to challenge his unhelpful and unconstructive thinking. You may have been able to devise others too. If so, please note them down.

What thoughts should Erik have had to remain goal-focused and not become so stressed? Instead of, 'This is awful. This should not be happening to me. Your airline is really useless,' a more realistic, goal-focused and problem-solving belief and attitude could be,

'This situation is a hassle but certainly not awful. I would strongly prefer this delay not to have occurred but as it has, tough, too bad. I can handle it. The airline may have flaws but this is hardly evidence that they are useless. I'll contact the office and inform them about the delay. I'll use the spare time to go over my presentation notes.'

Notice how each unhelpful belief was tackled individually. If Erik accepted the new self-helping belief instead of feeling anxious and angry, he would be more likely to feel concerned and annoyed which tend to be constructive emotions, enabling him to retain control of the situation.

Now consider how you could challenge your own self-defeating beliefs and attitudes that you may have found from the NTBQ. It is a good idea to ask yourself the question and then to spend a minute or two thinking about the issues it raises. Sometimes it is helpful to discuss these ideas with a friend who does not become stressed about travelling. Our approach will help you to think about your stress-inducing thinking. The list of challenging questions below developed by psychologists, Palmer and Strickland, may help.

Helpful challenging questions

- Is it logical?
- Would a scientist agree with my logic?
- Where is the evidence for my belief?
- Where is the belief written (apart from inside my own head)?
- Is my belief realistic?
- Would my friends and colleagues agree with my idea?
- Does everybody share my attitude? If not, why not?
- Am I expecting myself or others to be perfect as opposed to fallible human beings?

- What makes the situation so awful, terrible or horrible?
- Am I making a mountain out of a molehill?
- Will it seem this bad in one, three, six or twelve months time?
- Will it be important in two years time?
- Is it really as bad as a problem like a serious accident or a close bereavement?
- Am I exaggerating the importance of this problem?
- Am I fortune-telling again with little evidence that the worse case scenario will actually happen?
- If I 'can't stand it' or 'can't bear it' what will really happen?
- If I can't stand it, will I really fall apart?
- Am I concentrating on my (or others') weaknesses and neglecting my (or others') strengths?
- Am I agonising about how things should be instead of dealing with them as they are?
- Where is this thought or attitude getting me?
- Is my belief helping me to attain my goal(s)?
- Is my belief goal-focused and problem-solving?
- If a friend made a similar mistake would I be so critical?
- Am I thinking in all-or-nothing terms? Is there any middle ground?
- Am I labelling myself, somebody or something else? Is this logical and a fair thing to do?
- Just because a problem has occurred does it mean that I/they/it is stupid, a failure, useless or hopeless?
- Am I placing demands (eg. shoulds/musts etc.) on myself or others? If I am, is this proving helpful and constructive?

When you realise that you are becoming stressed, this is the time to stand back from the situation and tackle your negative beliefs. The art is to focus on the belief or attitude that seems to be exacerbating an already difficult situation.

These questions can also be used to gently challenge others' ideas if introduced carefully into the conversation. For example, when friends, colleagues and family members start becoming stressed about travelling often they will 'awfulise' or start to 'label' others. When this occurs you could ask them if the situation is really awful or just a hassle or whether the person is really useless or has just made an inconvenient error? This approach to challenging unhelpful beliefs was developed by the psychologist Dr Albert Ellis.

In this chapter we have focused on how negative beliefs and attitudes can contribute to our levels of stress in difficult situations. They wait to be triggered by external events. If travellers and holidaymakers recognise the beliefs before their journeys start, then their unhelpful ideas can be challenged and modified before their jaunt. *Chapter 4* will highlight additional techniques that can be used to help you in questioning your negative beliefs and attitudes.

2

Understanding fears, anxieties and phobias about flying

According to research between 9% and 33% of us have a fear of flying. Yet only 0.00001% of us will actually die in a plane crash (just in case you are not a mathematician, this is an extremely small percentage). Believe it or not, you stand a greater chance of being killed by lightning (0.00002% of the population each year). Accidents in the home or when crossing the road are far more likely. Given these statistics, why are so many people afraid or phobic of flying? This chapter will help you to understand fears, anxieties and phobias.

What is anxiety? What is a phobia?

Think back to the last time you felt anxious about someone or something. Perhaps you become anxious about travelling any distance from home or flying. Do you recognise any of the following symptoms.?

Psychological effects: how we think and feel

- apprehension
- nervousness
- alarm
- increased worrying
- lack of concentration
- unpleasant intrusive images or thoughts
- dread, fear
- terror
- helplessness
- racing thoughts
- inability to speak coherently

Physiological effects: how our body reacts

- breathlessness
- palpitations
- irregular heartbeat
- diarrhoea
- vomiting
- excessive sweating
- hairs on skin stand erect
- dry mouth
- numbing or tingling sensations in hands, or other extremities
- skin becomes pale
- rapid breathing
- pounding heartbeat
- blurred vision
- nausea, butterflies
- tightness in chest
- feeling faint
- heightened hearing
- tightness of throat
- trembling muscles, legs shake

Behavioural: how we behave

- avoidance
- clenched fists
- checking rituals
- biting nails/chewing hair
- urge to open the exits
- compulsive behaviour
- tapping foot
- agitation

These are some of the common symptoms of travelling and flying anxiety. In fact, anxiety and fear are similar. Fear is considered a normal response to a realistic threat. For example, most of us would be very frightened if we faced a charging elephant, yet only mildly anxious or concerned about giving a wedding speech in three months time. Some individuals actively seek or enjoy anxiety provoking situations such as parachuting, rock climbing and abseiling, and like the feelings and sensations that the activities trigger. In threatening situations, anxiety and fear can help a person survive as they galvanise the person into action. However, when people start to intensely fear or dread specific situations or things that are, in reality, nonthreatening, then they may have acquired a phobia. For example, being fearful of spiders in the United Kingdom would be considered irrational as dangerous ones do not exist in the wild and are mostly restricted to zoos and research establishments.

People usually decide to obtain professional help from doctors or psychologists about their phobias when they have to confront their problem on a regular basis or when they are prevented from achieving their goals. Travel or flying phobias are common and can interfere with social or work commitments. Often people with a phobia ask their doctor or psychologist: 'Am I going mad? Will I give it to my children? Am I normal?' Phobias do not drive people mad although they can be very frustrating. Even if children or other family members start to share similar worries, then they can be treated in the way we describe later in this chapter. People who suffer from phobias are 'normal' in the sense that many millions of people world-wide share their problem and, apart from their intense fear of a specific situation, object or animal, they are no different from the large majority of other humans in all other respects.

Characteristics of fears and phobias

Phobias are irrational; they cannot usually be explained or reasoned away and tend to be out of proportion to the feared situation. They may be extreme; they disrupt our life and lead to avoidance. They can be intrusive and occur when we least want them. Sometimes the fear is associated with shame; we worry that our reaction to the situation will be embarrassing or bring shame to us.

One important point to stress is that fears are relative.

After all, if everyone feared flying, there would be no pilots, cabin crew or passengers. Clearly, those who cope reasonably well with the experience of flying see and experience things differently to those who fear flying which, in turn, leads to different feelings. This raises two related questions: what causes a fear of flying and why is not everyone affected in the same way? There are several different causes of a fear of flying:

1. Lack of familiarity — the person is certain that if they fly, the plane will crash and they will die. They look at a plane and surmise that given, its weight and structure, it cannot possibly be supported or 'lifted' by moving air. The whole experience of flying frightens (or terrifies) them. If they have no option but to fly, they experience considerable anxiety before they travel (known as anticipatory anxiety), are distressed by any unfamiliar sounds in the cabin or turning motions, scrutinise the crew's faces for an indication that something is terribly wrong and seldom leave their seat during flight. Often these people have large gaps in their knowledge of how planes fly or a distorted information base about aeroplanes and flight.

2. Past experience of delays, turbulence, air sickness or aborted take-offs or landings may instil fear which becomes more pronounced when the person has to take another trip. This is in spite of the fact that they survived the unpleasant experience. The fear is that it will be repeated, or worse. Past traumatic experiences may or may not be linked to a fear of flying.

3. Lack of control — air travel involves placing trust in other skilled professionals. Almost every aspect of the experience reinforces this: we queue, wait, have to check-in, are separated

from luggage, may be delayed, are told where we are to be seated and when we can leave our seats, and so on. Feeling that we have little control in a situation can increase feelings of anxiety. People prone to suffering panic attacks also fear that they will lose control of their body. Some welcome a crash to end the extreme unpleasantness of the panic attack.

4. Claustrophobia is a fear of being trapped in a small or confined space, and aircraft cabins seem to trigger this fear in some people. It is made worse by the fact that the person feels they have no escape. After all, if they were in a bus, they could get out at the next stop. Fear increases in some people when they realise that they cannot ask the pilot to simply 'pull over' and let them out.

5. Acrophobia, or a fear of heights, can also present as a fear of flying. The person is terrified that there may be thousands of feet of 'empty space' between the ground and the plane and fear that turbulence or something else, will result in disaster. Interestingly, some people affected by this problem also fear moving around in the cabin because they perceive the floor to be fragile.

6. Those prone to thinking negatively — a recent life event such as a death, marriage, loss of a job or promotion at work can arouse people's emotions. Potentially stressful situations, such as air travel, can trigger feelings associated with anxiety as a form of emotional release. This in turn can lead to more intense feelings, sometimes associated with thinking negatively when coping with adversity. The person may not recognise the association between stressful life events and their fear and, instead, ask of themselves: 'Why is this

happening?' or 'Am I going crazy; this has never happened before?' These thoughts add to the person's worries as they challenge their self-perception that he or she can usually cope with stressful situations. Where no specific life event trigger can be identified, the fear may also be linked to another underlying psychological problem (such as depression). In a stress-susceptible personality, the fear may stem from low self-esteem, a lowered ability to take risks, perfectionism or catastrophic thinking.

7. Hereditary is a predisposing factor. There is an increased risk of having fears and suffering from anxiety and panic attacks where other family members are affected. This may be due to a genetic link or learned behaviour where events in a shared social environment conditions the person to a particular response or reaction to stress.

8. Childhood environment can also give rise to a range of fears, one of which may be associated with flying. Parents may be over-protective, controlling, or set impossibly high standards from which self-doubt and fears may arise. These may later lead to a fear of flying.

This list is by no means exhaustive and psychologists also recognise that a fear of flying can result from a combination of several of these possible causes. One symptom of fear is avoidance, this defence mechanism is sometimes helpful but it will not cure the problem. We cannot eradicate all fears and instead we should learn to understand, manage and control them. Using drugs or recreational drugs to mask the problem sometimes makes it worse because of the effects such stimulants have, during and after the threat of the situation has passed. Your fear of flying may, in fact, be more pronounced at this moment because your reading about it intensifies the feelings associated with fear in the short term. Harnessing some of the intense feelings associated with fear, and using these to motivate you to cope with your fear, is certainly a good thing.

Fear of flying triggers

Simply having a fear of flying is not usually sufficient to unleash unpleasant feelings. The fear needs a trigger or stimulus and this may come from one or more sources. Triggers reported to us by our clients include:

- booking a holiday or flight
- packing
- thinking about being on an aeroplane
- an incident report that is still fresh in our mind
- emotional arousal following a separation (saying goodbye to a loved one)
- physical sensations in the aeroplane (bank angle when turning or acceleration forces)
- noises in the aircraft cabin (engine, wind)
- smells in the aircraft cabin (aviation fuel, food)
- sights (unfamiliar ones such as the crew demonstrating safety procedures)
- a feeling of being outside the communication chain (crew talking among themselves, or air traffic control talking to the pilot, but information not being passed onto us).

In addition to these general triggers of anxiety, specific events or situations can feel worse when we try to interpret them. It is though a normal human response to try to understand and make sense of a situation. If it is something that gives cause for fear or instils anxiety, our interpretation of events may be distorted.

The distorted interpretation of each event in turn leads to specific feelings and behaviours, usually characterised by catastrophic or negative thinking. For example, a passenger might notice that the wings flex during turbulence. Their fear might be that they will snap off. In turn, they keep their eyes shut during turbulence and resist looking outside. Of course, while the fear is not unreasonable, it is based on incomplete or incorrect information. A new belief that we can introduce is that the wings are built to flex (it would be a very bumpy ride if they did not) when passing through different pressures and moving air. An alternative response (or behaviour) is to relax and look outside the window or calmly read a book.

Event	Distorted interpretation
Bumps from underneath the plane	The wheels have fallen off
Turning sensation	Avoiding a near collision; we're falling over
Reduction in speed	The engines are failing
Chime in the cabin	Crew are being summoned to an emergency briefing
Turbulence	The plane will fall apart
Shabby cabin interior	Lousy maintenance; this plane is not even air-worthy

Self-help: assessment

If you are scared or phobic of flying then it is always useful to discover what exactly you are frightened about. Psychologists call this procedure 'assessment'. For example, being very anxious about flying does not tell us whether you are actually anxious about take-off, landing, sitting in a small space, heights, falling through the floor, going mad or losing control. It is important to assess what precisely the problem is as it will affect how you can deal with or manage your fear or phobia. Questionnaires can help this process and can also tell us just how phobic you are compared to others.

Fear of flying survey (FFS)

The following Fear of Flying Survey (FFS) was originally published in a dissertation by SJ Solberg in 1975. Since then, it has been used at the Institute for the Psychology of Air Travel in Boston, USA and we are grateful to the director, Dr Forgione, who has given us permission to reproduce the survey in this book. On the FFS, beside each item, you can rate how frightened or bothered you are about each situation by using the following scale:

    0 = not at all
    1 = a little bit
    2 = a fair amount
    3 = much
    4 = very much

For example, for item 1 you would note down '2' if you felt that it bothered you 'a fair amount'.

When you undertake this exercise, if you start to feel very anxious then we suggest that you take a short break, especially if you encounter difficulty rating each item. (If you are prone to experiencing panic attacks or have a cardiac condition, then we would recommend that you undertake this exercise under medical or clinical supervision.)

Begin now to rate your anxiety or discomfort using the above scale on the items below.

1. You have decided to take a plane flight and you are at home making plane reservations and planning your trip   Rate:____

2. Your plane tickets arrive in the mail and you open the envelope and read the tickets.   Rate:____

3. It is the day of your flight and you are at home packing and preparing.   Rate:____

4. You leave home and drive to the airport.   Rate:____

5. You arrive at the airport and go to the appropriate airline, where you check your baggage and are assigned a seat.   Rate:____

6. You pass through the security check and metal detector where you are checked by the security guard.   Rate:____

7. You are in the departure area at the gate and, as you sit, you are aware of the activity of other people coming and going on other flights.   Rate:____

8. Your flight number is called and you gather your hand luggage and get in line to enter the plane.   Rate:____

9. You walk onto the plane and are greeted by the flight attendant. You notice the interior of the plane with its rows of seats and small windows. Rate:_____

10. You walk down the aisle until you find your seat. You put your hand luggage in the overhead compartment and settle into your seat. Rate:_____

11. You realise that the aircraft door is shut and you cannot leave the plane. Rate:_____

12. Your plane is on the ground prior to take-off. It is a stormy, rainy day. Looking out of the window, you see sheets of rain pouring down and see puddles of water forming on the runway. Rate:_____

13. You feel the first lurch as the plane begins to move toward the runway. Rate:_____

14. As the plane moves toward the runway, the flight attendant demonstrates the use of the oxygen mask, seat belt and gives other safety instructions. Rate:_____

15. As you wait for the plane to take off, the flight attendant walks down the aisle checking if the seat belts are fastened. You reach down and check your seat belt. Rate:_____

16. Your plane has been given permission to take off and it begins to pick up speed rapidly as it moves down the runway. You feel the vibrations and hear the engines roar. Rate:_____

17. As the plane lifts off the ground, you hear the 'thump' of the landing gear as it is retracted. Rate:_____

18. As the plane climbs, you feel the push back- Rate:____
ward into your seat and the small changes in
air pressure and the vibrations as the plane cuts
through the air.

19. You are flying at a steady altitude in calm Rate:____
weather.

20. You are in flight and look out of the window Rate:____
and see the panorama below. Everything looks
small below your view high above.

21. You are on a long flight and, glancing at your Rate:____
watch, figure that four more hours of flight are
left.

22. While the plane is in flight, the pilot Rate:____
announces that the plane is behind schedule
and will arrive 30 minutes late.

23. You are flying in dense fog. When you look Rate:____
out of the window you can see nothing but
thick fog; you cannot even see the wing tip.

24. Your plane encounters turbulence. The flight Rate:____
becomes rough and bouncy and you are re-
quired to fasten your seat belt.

25. Unexpectedly, the plane encounters a down- Rate:____
draft (an 'air pocket'). You feel a great jolt as
the plane suddenly changes altitude. The jolt
causes confusion and disorder as passengers
are thrown off balance and loose objects are
knocked out of place.

26. Your plane is approaching its destination and the 'fasten seat belt' sign flashes on. You feel a change in air pressure as the plane starts to descend.   Rate:_____

27. As the plane descends for landing, the wing flaps are lowered causing the plane to vibrate a little. You hear the 'thump' of the landing gear being lowered and the plane vibrates.   Rate:_____

28. As the plane touches down, and begins moving down the runway, you hear the roar and feel the plane vibrate as you are pushed forward when the pilot reverses the thrust of the engines to slow the plane.   Rate:_____

29. Your flight is over. Your plane taxis to the place where you will disembark.   Rate:_____

30. Thinking about the flight three weeks before the scheduled date.   Rate:_____

31. Thinking about the flight the weekend before the scheduled date.   Rate:_____

32. Thinking about the flight the week before the scheduled date.   Rate:_____

33. Thinking about the flight the night before the scheduled date.   Rate:_____

34. Thinking about the flight the hour before take-off.   Rate:_____

35. Talking with friends about flying.   Rate:_____

36. Going to the airport to see friends or relatives off on a flight. Rate:_____

37. In a plane flying over mountains. Rate:_____

38. In a plane flying over the ocean. Rate:_____

39. In a plane flying on a clear day. Rate:_____

40. In a plane flying at night. Rate:_____

41. In a plane flying in winter. Rate:_____

42. Watching planes take-off and land. Rate:_____

43. Eating a meal during a flight. Rate:_____

44. Having my family on the plane with me during the flight. Rate:_____

45. Flying on a plane by myself (without friends or relatives). Rate:_____

46. Flying on a plane with a friend sitting next to me. Rate:_____

To find out how phobic you are, all you need to do is to total the rating scores for the entire FFS. The maximum score you can obtain is 184. When the Institute for the Psychology of Air Travel undertook a research programme with 4000 fearful flyers they found that about 20% scored between 150 and 183, and 3% scored a maximum of 184. The ranges of scores for calmer fliers, who do not identify themselves as fearful fliers, and fearful fliers are illustrated in *Table 2.1*.

Table 2.1			
	FFS Score	**3926 Fearful**	**467 Calmer**
Phobia	184–150	22%	0.03%
Intense fear	149–100	38%	0.42%
Moderate fear	99–50	27%	14.4%
Mild fear	49–25	12%	34.28%
Negligible fear	24–00	1%	50.9%

The Institute discovered that the calmer fliers flew three or more times (one-way trips) in the preceding year, while the fearful respondents flew an average of 0.2 flights in the preceding year. This is an interesting observation as it implies that by avoiding flying, the fearful fliers continued to stay frightened about flying. In other words, only by facing fears do people, or in this case fliers, become more confident about flying. Perhaps this is why if one falls off a horse or a bicycle, it is always recommended to get back on immediately to help overcome any fears that may develop about riding. Notice that the Institute found that even a larger number of calmer fliers had some degree of apprehension, while 87% of the fearful fliers had scores above 50. No wonder the research shows that between 9% and 33% of the population are fearful of flying and 15% to 18% actually avoid flying.

One of the key issues with irrational fears and phobias is anticipatory anxiety. If a person is extremely worried about travelling by plane, then his or her exaggerated negative thinking and images about flying will trigger such high levels of anxiety that the person can avoid flying altogether. This is a clear example of a phobia.

You can use the FFS to assess how much anticipatory anxiety you suffer from. Add up the total scores for the anticipatory items: 1, 2, 3, 4, 5, 6, 7, 8, 30, 31, 32, 33, 34, 35, 36, 42.

You can compare your score with the fliers on the research programme at the Institute for the Psychology of Air Travel in *Table 2.2.*

Table 2.2		
	Non-fliers/ fearful fliers	**Calmer fliers**
Average anticipatory score	41.3	5.8
Average common flying score	51.1	21.4

These figures highlight that non-fliers and fearful fliers experience a high level of anticipatory anxiety. This leaves non-fliers and fearful fliers a clear option and training plan: reduce their anticipatory anxiety. Fearful fliers who do not deal with this could even become phobic if they allow their anticipatory anxiety to worsen.

Case study

Sara had never liked flying. Days before going on holiday she would become steadily more anxious, thinking about her plane crashing. Usually the night before take-off, if she did manage to get to sleep, she would have a nightmare about the plane crashing. On this particular trip she was returning home to London, with her partner, from a holiday in Milan. To cope with her anxiety, she would drink a fair number of alcoholic beverages. Unfortunately, over the Alps the plane experienced turbulence and this triggered her first panic attack. She felt totally out of control and felt so bad that she thought she was going to have a heart attack and die. This convinced her that flying was dangerous and she refused to fly again. She told her partner, 'I feel so anxious about flying. It must be dangerous'.

This case study illustrates how easily high levels of anxiety can lead to a panic attack and subsequently the person can become phobic of flying. Notice how Sara used emotional reasoning: 'I feel so anxious about flying. It must be dangerous'. Emotional reasoning in which travellers base their assessment of danger on how anxious they feel is usually empirically incorrect and not based on the facts. It is worth noting that Sara is unlikely to have suffered the panic attack in the first place if she had not made herself so fearful with her anticipatory anxiety and pictures in her mind of the plane crashing prior to the flight.

Incidentally, did you notice the trick item in the FFS? Most people would score 4 for item number 25. If you scored less you may wish to re-examine your honesty when taking this test.

Panic attacks

So, what is a panic attack? Typically, people who fear flying report a range of worries which include: being in an enclosed space, feeling anxious if there is turbulence during the flight, the threat of bombs and hijacks, delays, being away from home, the take-off and landing phases of flight, as well as customs, baggage reclaim and many others. They also describe unpleasant physical symptoms associated with some of these fears, including nausea, dizziness, diarrhoea, breathlessness, headaches and a pounding heart. These symptoms are sometimes so intense that they lead to the additional worry; that the person is physically unwell and could need urgent medical assistance.

Feelings of panic, of course, make the experience feel much worse: this could then lead to a full blown panic attack which can feel frightening. The following flow chart (*Figure 2.1*) illustrates another example of how a simple fear can lead to a panic attack.

Figure 2.1: Evolution of a panic attack

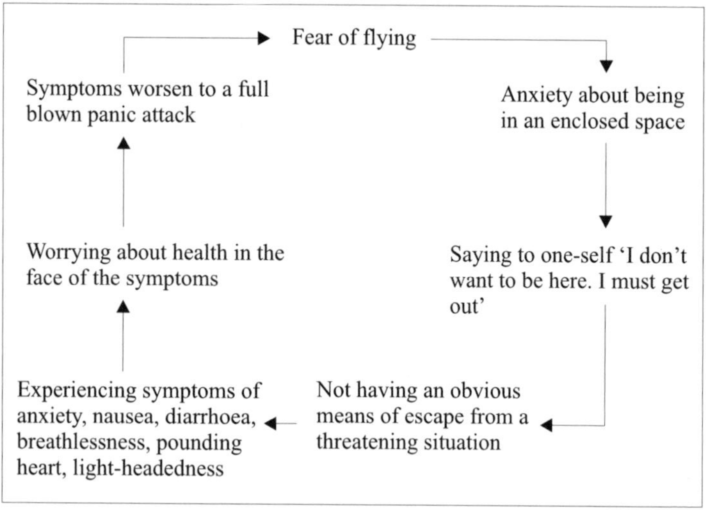

Specific fears associated with flying are common, even among seasoned fliers. The difference is that they cope better with their fears which increases their confidence. This chapter can be the catalyst that facilitates this process by helping you to understand the causes of fears and anxieties associated with flying. In the next chapter we focus on how you can develop your own self-help training programme to reduce, manage or conquer your flying-related fears, anxieties and phobias.

3

Conquering fears and anxieties about flying: a self-help tool kit

In *Chapter 2*, you were able to assess exactly what you become stressed about when travelling or thinking of travelling. This chapter offers a tool kit of methods and techniques that may help you to overcome moderate to high levels of flying anxiety and flying phobia. The chapter starts with a number of areas about flying that are often misunderstood by nervous travellers.

Reduce stress by understanding the facts about flying

Often passengers do not understand how planes fly and, generally, have fears about engines failing and turbulence. By increasing their knowledge of these issues, we have found that many have managed to reduce their fears and anxieties about flying. Below we consider six common fears expressed by passengers.

Why does the plane sometimes feel as if it is 'sinking' for a short while after take-off?

Most large airports are situated in close proximity to cities or built up areas. Airports are usually subjected to noise control regulations. Shortly after take-off, the pilot may be required to reduce engine power for a few minutes to conform to these noise pollution rules. The sensation that often accompanies this is one of sinking or falling. In fact, the plane is still climbing but at a slightly shallower rate though the reduction in engine noise may make you believe that there is something wrong. This is a common and normal experience. You could be forewarned if you pop your head into the flight deck when you board and ask the pilots whether they will be reducing power after take-off for 'noise abatement' reasons.

Why do planes feel as if they are falling over when they turn?

The short answer is to make changing direction more comfortable. It is similar to when you turn a corner in a car; if you lean into the direction of the turn, you feel less resistance in your body. Large commercial aircraft rarely make steep turns similar to those you may have seen practised by aerobats. The angle of bank (as a turn is called) is seldom more than 30 degrees but, because of the size of the plane and the sensitivity of the balance mechanism in your ear, it can feel more than that.

What if an engine fails?

Aircraft engines are among the most expensive and sophisticated parts of a plane. Nowadays, they are extremely reliable. Aircraft and engine manufacturers are generally very cautious people and, even though the chances of a problem are remote, the crew are thoroughly trained to cope with this eventuality. No commercial plane can be licensed unless it can be demonstrated that the plane can keep flying with only one engine operating. In such a situation, the pilot would obviously land as soon as possible as a precaution. In the unlikely situation of all engines failing, the plane would become a glider and gradually float down to earth. Remember, the plane has height, forward momentum and loads of air to keep it up for a while. At cruising height (35,000 feet) it could take up to half an hour to glide down in which time everyone could be prepared for the landing.

What is turbulence and why is it sometimes scary?

Turbulence, or 'bumpiness' as it is sometimes called, occurs when the plane passes through strong wind currents. These are similar to ocean currents. Remember that planes do not fly in a vacuum; air supports them (or gives them a lift) and air is seldom stationary. From watching the weather report on television, you will see that the wind strength and direction is usually given or marked on the weather map. Because most commercial planes fly so high, they are above most of the weather which is likely to cause turbulence. You are more likely to encounter some turbulence when flying at lower altitudes and speeds, such as during take-off and landing. However, you may encounter fast moving air masses, such as the 'jet stream', at higher altitudes. If you are heading in the same direction as the jet stream, it could be hugely advantageous and considerably reduce your flying time. Most modern commercial planes can detect turbulence on special radar systems, which is why the pilots may sometimes ask passengers to remain seated with their seatbelts fastened even before any turbulence is encountered. Some turbulence (such as clear air turbulence) may be undetectable and, unless a pilot in another plane has alerted his or her colleagues to this, it may come unexpectedly.

It is important to remember that that turbulence is seldom dangerous. Planes can withstand huge forces. Perhaps the sight of the wings flexing in the turbulent conditions will trigger anxiety, but think of the wings as shock absorbers that dampen the movements caused by turbulent air. It makes the ride more comfortable. There is no risk of the wings 'breaking off'; they are not flimsily attached to the sides of the plane. Think of the wings as one long single structure on which we ride (in the cabin). Cabin crew may stop serving food and drinks when it becomes turbulent because there is the obvious risk of spillage and the pilots may require you to remain seated for your protection. Once again, turbulence may feel uncomfortable, but it is seldom dangerous.

What if the pilot becomes ill?

This scenario was recently depicted in comedy. However, the worry cannot easily be fobbed off with humour. Fortunately, there is almost always a minimum of two flight crew (pilots) on commercial flights and, on some long-haul trips, up to six. If one member of the crew becomes unwell, there is always someone who can relieve him/her. Flight crew eat entirely different meals to guard against this eventuality as gastrointestinal problems are among the most common ailments from which they suffer. Operating procedures require pilots to divert to the nearest airport if one of the crew, or passengers, for that matter, becomes unwell. Safety is the most important aspect of air travel and no chances are ever taken. Crew also have to meet strict medical requirements and are regularly assessed by doctors to ensure that they are in good health. Their retirement age is also lower than that found in most other occupations.

How does all that heavy metal stay up in the air?

The quick answer is: the aerodynamic shape of the structure, air and thrust. The unique shape of the plane and the wing size provide a huge amount of lift. The next time you are driving onto a motorway, imagine what would happen if you stuck your arm out of the window when travelling at high speed (do note that we are not suggesting that you actually put your arm out of the window). Your arm would have to resist a large amount of pressure from the air and would probably also rise. This is almost exactly what happens to a plane. Moving air provides lift to the wings and, at a certain point while accelerating down the runway, the plane simply cannot stay on the ground. The powerful engines provide the forward motion (or thrust). Even if the engines are switched off in flight, forward motion is maintained through momentum resulting in a gradual decline or loss of height. Even though planes can be very heavily laden with passengers, fuel, baggage, cargo and, of course, the weight of the structure, the three factors listed — shape, air and thrust — make flight possible. The crew carefully calculate how much fuel, power and runway length are needed for the plane to take off before each flight. This explains why you are unlikely to see the pilots walking around the cabin when you board as they are busy with their calculations and checking all the instruments and systems. The principles of flight are the same for any aircraft. If you get the chance, visit your local flying school and ask an instructor to explain these ideas in more detail. You may even be encouraged to go on your first trial flying lesson.

Once anxious passengers understand these six points they can start to challenge their misunderstandings in a structured and constructive manner. It is usually a good idea to write down the belief or misunderstanding, noting your feelings and behaviour. Then the new belief, based on knowledge, is noted down which helps to change a person's feelings and behaviour. Two examples are provided in *Table 3.1* and *Table 3.2*.

Table 3.1			
Belief/ inaccurate information	**Feelings/ behaviour**	**New belief**	**New feelings/ behaviour**
Walking around the cabin unbalances the plane	Muscles tighten, stay in seat, grip arm-rests; anxious	Planes are stabilised by the wings; they do not tip over	Relax, walk around, watch what happens when others walk around

Table 3.2			
Belief/ inaccurate information	**Feelings/ behaviour**	**New belief**	**New feelings/ behaviour**
If the engine fails, the plane will fall out of the sky and crash	Filled with anxiety, the person listens for any change in the engine sound anticipating that they will stop	Most passenger planes have several engines; they can fly without some working; if all fail, the plane turns into a glider and gently descends	Enjoy the in-flight movie. Just as the engine sounds different when we accelerate or decelerate in our car, so the same happens in the flight

These examples illustrate the value of having some knowledge about planes and flying. If you still feel anxious about flying it is recommended that you consider using one or more strategies from the following sections.

Graded exposure

Extensive research has found that if a person stays in contact (known as exposure) with the feared situation, after a period of time his or her anxiety starts to lessen (*Figure 3.1*).

Figure 3.1: Typical effect of exposure

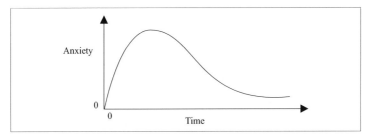

Graded exposure is exposure to feared situations in manageable steps. A person who is anxious about flying would initially be exposed to those fears that trigger their anticipatory anxiety in their imagination before exposure in real life to flying. This approach is normally effective unless the person undergoing the training programme is depressed, has drunk two or more units of alcohol prior or during the exposure exercise, or is taking sedatives such as valium.

Have another look at your completed FFS (see *pages*

24–28). Highlight the key items where you scored from one to four, in other words those you were bothered about from 'a fair amount' to 'very much' (these are known as subjective units of distress). Then put them in order of how stressed you are by the individual items. This is called 'ranking'. Maggie ranked her key items as follows (see *Table 3.3*).

Rank	Subjective units of distress	Event/item
	Table 3.3: Maggie's hierarchy of fears	
1	4	23 (dense fog)
2	4	24 (turbulence)
3	4	18 (feeling the push backward)
4	4	17 (hear thump of landing gear as it is retracted)
5	4	16 (plane picks up speed)
6	4	27 (plane descends)
7	4	40 (flying at night)
8	3	28 (plane touches down)
9	3	15 (checking seat belt)
10	3	13 (first lurch as plane moves)
11	3	11 (aircraft door is shut)
12	2	43 (eating a meal)
13	2	8 (get in line to enter plane)
14	1	5 (checking baggage)
15	1	4 (leaving home and driving to the airport)

Although Maggie also rated the other items on the FFS, the 15 included in her hierarchy of fears were the ones that she felt most anxious about. How she devised her own exposure programme to reduce her anticipatory anxiety is illustrated as follows.

Case study

Maggie, an academic, suffered from flying phobia. She had only flown once before and had become very anxious. Since that time she had always avoided travelling by plane. However, she wanted to attend an important international conference in New Zealand and going by sea was out of the question as it would take far too long. A long haul flight was the only answer. Maggie decided that she would start her graded exposure programme (in her imagination) at her ranking of 13, which felt uncomfortable but not overwhelming. She sat comfortably in the armchair in her sitting room. She closed her eyes and imagined that her flight was being called, she was gathering her hand luggage and getting into line to enter the plane. After about 10 minutes, instead of feeling a fair amount of anxiety, she only felt a little anxious. In other words, her rating went down from two to one. She then imagined the next item going up the list which had a ranking of 12, ie. eating a meal during a flight. Again, after about 10 minutes, she felt only a little bit anxious so she started with the next item on the list. However, imagining the aircraft door shutting and not being able to leave the plane took longer for her to get used to as it triggered a great deal of anxiety (three on our scale). After about 10 minutes her anxiety went down to two (a fair amount) but it took another 12 minutes before it dropped to one (a little bit.) Not surprisingly, she felt tired after this exercise. The next day she returned to it and started again at her ranking of 11, the door shutting, just to ensure that she had conquered this anticipatory fear. Then she continued up the list. By her third day of working on this, she was able to cope with imagining flying in dense fog and not being able to see the wing tip. On the fourth day she was even able to tolerate imagining flying through dense fog and experiencing turbulence simultaneously while eating a meal.

This was just the initial phase of Maggie's self-help training programme. Her anticipatory anxiety had now subsided and she was thinking far less about the forthcoming journey. By visiting her local airport prior to her trip, although again her anxiety increased to three on our zero to four scale, just by watching and listening to the planes taking off and landing, her anxiety subsided and varied between zero to one on our scale within an hour of undertaking this exercise. This real life exposure exercise really helped to build up her confidence. She also recorded on a video recorder planes taking off and landing so that she could watch and listen to the video in the comfort of her home to ensure that she had her anxieties under control.

Modifying beliefs and thought stopping

In *Chapter 1* we covered a number of negative travel beliefs that unfortunately increase our stress levels. You may wish to return to the Negative Travel Beliefs Questionnaire (NTBQ) on *page 3* and re-examine the beliefs that you hold strongly. There are a number of negative beliefs that tend to trigger high levels of anxiety as well as being associated with phobias. These are:

10. I/we must not encounter problems.
18. I/we must be in control of all situations.

20.   If things go badly then it would be 'awful'.
21.   If things go badly then I could not stand it.
22.   Things never go well on my trips and holidays.

Include any additional beliefs that you may have noted down for number 24. *Chapter 1* demonstrated how you can challenge these beliefs and develop more helpful beliefs, such as:

10.   It is strongly preferable not to encounter problems but, if we do, it is not the end of the world.

18.   Although it is preferable to be in control of all situations, it is not essential.

20.   Things are seldom 'awful' or life horrors. Generally, they are just a life hassle.

21.   I'm living proof that when things have gone badly in the past I have survived. This is more evidence that I can stand things.

22.   Although occasionally things may go wrong, seldom (if ever) does everything go wrong on my trips and holidays. This is just all or nothing thinking again.

Another strategy for dealing with negative beliefs is to use thought stopping to actually bring a train of thought to a halt. As soon as a negative belief or prediction is considered by the traveller, it can be disrupted by snapping an elastic band which has been placed on the wrist.

Case study

One of John's worst fears was that the plane would crash. On the journey, when the plane experienced turbulence, John suddenly thought of it crashing. He immediately snapped the elastic band to halt this negative prediction and reminded himself of a previously prepared self-helping statement: 'It's just turbulence. Planes hardly ever crash'. Later, when the plane was coming into land, John had to repeat the process again to control his anxiety and fear that the plane would crash.

Other travellers who have obsessive negative thoughts have found that practising thought control before the flight can be extremely useful.

Case study

Mary was experiencing great difficulty in controlling her obsessive thoughts about dying while on her next long haul flight to the USA. She suffered from claustrophobia and thought that she would feel hemmed in and, perhaps, even die. She undertook a step by step approach. Initially she invoked her negative thought, 'I feel hemmed in. I'm going to die'. Then she clapped her hands loudly and simultaneously shouted out 'stop'. This helped to disrupt her negative train of thought. Then she invoked her negative thought again but this time did not clap or shout quite so loudly, again this helped to stop her thoughts. She repeated this process until she did not have to make any external noise at all. She discovered that just saying the word 'stop' very loudly in her head was sufficient to stop her negative obsessive thoughts.

Some travellers find the use of imagery very helpful in stopping their negative thoughts, especially those who tend to think with catastrophic pictures.

Case study

Whenever Felix thought about flying he would see pictures in his mind of the plane crashing. He had tried thought stopping but found that simply saying 'STOP' was insufficient to disrupt his catastrophic images. However, he found another method far more useful. As soon as the image of the plane crashing intruded, he pictured huge neon signs flashing 'stop' repeatedly on and off. On every occasion, when he had the negative picture he would literally intercept it by applying this method. After some practice he started to intervene without even thinking about what he was doing; by then it had become almost habitual.

Often nervous travellers have to find their own safe method of stopping their negative thoughts and/or pictures. If you find the methods discussed here are not particularly helpful we recommend that you experiment with your own adaptation.

Coping imagery

One of the most important methods used to reduce flying stress is known as coping imagery. This is in contrast to the negative and catastrophic imagery that flying phobics naturally use before and during a flight which triggers high levels of anxiety and even panic. Typical negative imagery is of planes crashing, looking foolish, losing control, going crazy, passengers vomiting, screaming and dying. Is it any wonder that passengers find it difficult to relax.

In coping imagery the would-be traveller pictures him or herself coping or dealing adequately with the feared situation. There is a simple five step approach to help you devise your coping imagery.

Step 1:   Think about the impending journey.

Step 2:   Identify the aspects of the journey that you are most anxious about.

Step 3:   Think of ways to overcome these problems.

Step 4:   Now visualise yourself undertaking the entire journey, coping with the problems you are anxious about.

Step 5:   Practise this coping imagery regularly, especially every time you begin to feel anxious about the forthcoming journey.

If you encounter difficulties developing strategies to deal with the predicted problems, consider how experienced travellers would deal with them, or ask a colleague or friend who is a seasoned traveller to give you some ideas. In our earlier case study, Maggie found coping imagery gave her a clearer idea how to deal with flying.

Although Maggie had found the imaginable and real life exposure really helped to reduce her anticipatory anxiety, she was still unsure how she was going to deal with any problems that might occur on the journey. With the help of an experienced traveller, she wrote down the key events about her proposed journey and included ways to deal with problems that they suggested might arise:

- Pre-flight planning — prepare itinerary
- Pack bags, conference papers, ticket and passport the night before take-off — check itinerary
- Booking taxi — use reliable company
- Going to bed — ensure early night
- Waking up, getting washed, dressed and having breakfast — prepare clothes and breakfast the evening before
- Locking up the house and getting into the taxi with bags, conference papers, ticket and passport — no problem
- Getting stuck in the inevitable traffic jam near Heathrow airport — stay calm, breathe slowly. Remind myself that I left in plenty of time

- Arriving at Heathrow at the correct terminal, paying the taxi driver and unloading all of my baggage — have some Sterling available
- Checking in — ask for aisle seat
- Possibly anxious about waiting — drink a cup of tea at a bar to help relax and collect thoughts. Avoid alcohol
- Unsure about boarding times — check times of the flight on the board
- Going through customs, showing passport and having hand holdall searched — stay calm; they are only doing their job
- Looking at the goods in the duty free shops — remember, only purchase what I need
- Check the board about my flight and go to the correct gate — no problem
- Waiting for a while and then boarding the plane — remind myself that it is more dangerous crossing the road than boarding a plane
- Being greeted by the cabin crew and making my way to the seat, hopefully an aisle one — look forward to the journey
- Putting holdall in the cupboard above the seat — no problem
- Making myself comfortable in my seat and putting on my seat belt and adjusting it — no problem, done this before
- Plane door closes — read to take my mind off things
- Engine starts. Taxiing down the runway; brakes squeak — remember that it is normal for brakes to squeak
- Safety announcements and cabin crew demonstrating how to use the life jacket — pay close attention
- Hear the plane flaps extending — this is supposed to happen

- Cabin staff asked to 'prepare for take-off'
- Single chime sounds
- Plane accelerating down the runway, with the occasional bump — either look out of the window to see the view or carry on reading
- Gently pushed into my seat by the acceleration — remind myself that this is quite normal
- Another thump as the wheels extend
- Plane lifts off with a roar — the plane engines have to be noisy to ensure we take off
- Thumping noises as the landing gear is raised and whining noises of the flaps as they are retracted – this means that the flight is going well
- More pressure pushing me back into the seat. Stomach may feel odd — carry on reading
- Plane reduces power and starts to level off slightly
- Chime sounds once at 1500 feet
- Chime sounds once at 10,000 feet
- Eventually plane levels off and engine noise decreases — remind myself that there is nothing wrong. This is supposed to happen
- Chime sounds and seat belt sign is turned off
- Captain announces that the seat sign is now off although it is still recommended that seat belts should be fastened when seated. We will cruise at 33,000 feet
- Drinking and eating food
- Experience turbulence. Chime sounds for fastening seat belts. Plane appears to shake. Other passengers look worried — remind myself that it is only turbulence and not dangerous. We

would be extremely unlucky if the plane crashed! May as well continue reading

- Turbulence finishes
- On the descent, plane enters dense cloud and I become unable to see the wing tips out of the window — remind myself that the Captain uses radar so this is unimportant
- Captain announces that due to the amount of traffic there will be a slight delay — remind myself that this does not mean that the situation is dangerous
- Chime at 10,000 feet
- Slight turbulence during descent — remind myself that this is to be expected and is not dangerous. I may as well continue to read
- Fasten seat belt
- Ears may pop — this is normal
- Flaps groan into life — we are preparing to land, that is all
- Cabin crew asked to prepare for landing
- Thumping noises as landing gear is lowered — if we didn't hear this then there would be a problem
- Engines become very loud — nothing to worry about
- Bumpy touch-down due to poor weather conditions — remind myself that planes seldom crash
- Flaps groaning again
- Loud engine noise as engines go into reverse to stop the plane — remind myself that this noise is quite normal and we will be stopping very soon
- Brakes squeaking
- Plane, thankfully, slows down very rapidly — relief

- Lights flicker — changing over to reserve systems
- Cabin crew asked to prepare the doors
- Announcement asks passengers to stay seated
- Chime sounds: seat belt sign off
- Unfasten seat belt, get holdall from locker, and queue to get off plane
- Follow directions to get baggage and go through customs
- Pick up a taxi and go to hotel.

Once she had noted down this extensive list she then read it very slowly, imagining in her mind's eye (and ears) each step of the journey. At the difficult steps, such as experiencing turbulence, she said out aloud her coping statements, eg. 'This is only turbulence. It is not dangerous'. She repeated this process daily and found time to do it in the taxi on the way to the airport and while she was having a cup of tea at the bar when she was collecting her thoughts. The outcome was that she experienced little anxiety on the entire journey.

To make the process easier, coping imagery can also be recorded onto an audio cassette to help you imagine the journey with your eyes closed. Although you may find Maggie's coping imagery useful, many nervous travellers find that they have to adapt parts of it to help them deal with their particular fear. For example, some travellers' worst fear is vomiting in the aisle. If this is your problem, you need to include in the coping imagery how you would deal with this situation.

Time projection imagery

During a flight, if you become very anxious about the turbulence that the plane may be experiencing or some other unpleasant event, then time projection imagery is a useful technique. The traveller imagines the future once he or she has safely landed and this helps to put his/her current problem into perspective.

Case study

Fran was on a trip from the USA to New Zealand and over the Pacific her plane experienced quite severe turbulence. She started to imagine that the plane was going to crash into the sea. This picture triggered high levels of anxiety. She remembered what a friend had told her, 'Worrying only achieves more worry and seldom seems to help any situation'. She then started to imagine that she had already arrived in New Zealand and had taken the internal flight down to Wellington. She then imagined going out with her family and friends to one of her favourite restaurants in town. She told them how she had unnecessarily distressed herself worrying about the plane crashing, even though she knew that it was extremely rare for turbulence to cause a crash.

By seeing herself in the future, laughing at her current worries and also enjoying herself, helped Fran to relax and ignore the turbulence.

Positive relaxation imagery

Positive relaxation imagery helps to reduce physical and emotional tension. The following exercise involves picturing a pleasant scene, such as your favourite relaxing place. Every-body usually has their own real or imaginary place, such as being in a garden, walking in a wood, sunbathing, or taking a hot bath.

Step 1:   If possible, reduce the level of lighting.

Step 2:   Make yourself comfortable. Recline in the chair.

Step 3:   Close your eyes. (Perhaps use an eyeshade.)

Step 4:   Imagine a favourite place where you feel relaxed.

Step 5:   Focus on the colours in your relaxing place.

Step 6:   Now focus on one colour.

Step 7:   Now focus on the sounds or silence.

Step 8:   Now focus on any aromas or smells.

Step 9:   Now imagine touching something.

Step 10:   When you are ready, open your eyes.

It is important to practise this exercise on a regular basis so that when you are feeling stressed it is not difficult to use success-fully. A simple analogy would be going for a driving test after having no driving lessons. In these circumstances you would be extremely likely to fail your test. Likewise, if you only use positive relaxation imagery when you are feeling anxious or angry you are likely to experience difficulties in its application. It is a very easy technique to learn and can also help travellers with sleeping difficulties.

Benson relaxation

Many travellers find it helpful to use a modern form of meditation developed by Dr Benson to reduce stress. This advanced, but simple method has also been shown to reduce blood pressure. Palmer and Strickland (1996) use the following seven step approach to teaching the method:

Step 1:   Make yourself as comfortable as possible in your seat.

Step 2:   Close your eyes.

Step 3:   Relax your muscles in groups, starting at your face and progressing down to your toes.

Step 4:   Now focus on your breathing. Breathe naturally through your nose. Imagine that your breathing is coming from your stomach (ie. diaphragmatic breathing). Avoid letting your shoulders rise.

Step 5:   Choose a number, perhaps the number 'one'. In your mind, say the number every time you breathe out.

Step 6:   Continue for 8–20 minutes. If distracting thoughts occur, just ignore them and return to repeating the number.

Step 7:   Finish in your own time. Keep your eyes closed for a couple of minutes and sit quietly.

It is not a good idea to try too hard to relax. Just let the process occur naturally. You may need to practise this method a number of times before you feel comfortable. Between Steps 6 and 7 you can introduce coping or time projection imagery to help you deal with difficult situations.

A final series of hints and suggestions to help you to cope with a fear of flying:

- do not avoid dealing with the problem, but seek help early

- get used to the sights, sounds, routine and smells of airports; visit one
- avoid drinking tea/coffee/alcohol or using tranquillisers as they can make you feel worse; discuss your fear with your doctor and ask whether he or she would consider prescribing a beta-blocker to help with the symptoms of anxiety
- talk to your neighbour on board the aircraft; it breaks the spell
- tell a flight attendant that you have a fear of flying
- remember to do deep diaphragmatic breathing to relax
- distract yourself
- remember that turbulence may feel uncomfortable, although is seldom dangerous.

4

How to survive air terminals

For most people, the excitement and anxiety of travel begins long before leaving home. Eager anticipation can easily evaporate after a stressful journey to the airport, followed by arrival at an air terminal filled with noise, confusion and crowds of people. This chapter describes the unique environment of the air terminal and the stresses such an environment induces, as well as strategies to help you cope. To set the scene, try to think of your last plane trip. Even if you are a confident traveller, it is likely that you experienced some hassle either getting to the airport, or having to wait for the bus to the terminal after parking your car, queueing to check in, and so on. Your arrival at the air terminal may thus be preceded by feelings of annoyance or anxiety. The design and layout of the terminal may increase any stress assuming, of course, that you have reached the right terminal. Terminals are self-enclosed, artificially heated or air-conditioned, noisy, busy and usually unfamiliar environments in which you are bombarded with visual and auditory stimuli, which may or may not be comprehensible. For some travellers, the worries associated with airports stem from the lack of familiarity as well as the design of air terminals; for others, the difficulties are more closely related to psychological factors. The following list includes some common problems associated with air terminals and some suggested coping strategies.

Getting there: with the huge increase in air travel and the increase in car traffic on the feeder roads to many airports, the first major hurdle is to get to the airport on time. Additionally, many large cities have several airports in their vicinity and you need to make sure you are making your way to the right airport. Once at the airport, you have to get to the correct terminal. Any potential stress induced by getting to the airport can be largely eliminated by planning and allowing plenty of time. It is usually possible to obtain information about the state of the roads prior to leaving home. The internet or a good travel agent can provide you with information about the state and business of roads near airports overseas.

Size and quantity of luggage: despite the frequently given advice in the media to pack only the essentials, most of us are guilty of taking far too much. A suitcase which seemed manageable at the beginning of a trip can often appear to have grown much heavier by the end of a trip. But the anxiety about not having enough, or forgetting to take something, can override any logic about making realistic assessments of the quantity of luggage needed. Separation from one's own luggage can cause worry. Some airlines are more reliable than others in ensuring that luggage reaches the same destination as the traveller and at the same time. However, practical solutions can help ameliorate many luggage problems. For example, many suitcases now have wheels but you still need to watch the weight as help is not always to hand to lift your case. Do not be afraid to ask for help if you need it, particularly as some smaller airports do not have luggage trolleys. When packing your suitcase, both to minimise your stress and reduce the volume, it can be helpful to ask yourself, 'Do I really need this, when would I wear/use it, does it crease, what is the worst that would happen if I did not pack this item?' Most airlines now have a prescribed size for hand luggage and again it can be helpful if it has wheels as the distances you have to walk in different airports vary hugely. Older and less mobile people may need to take precautions and ask for a wheelchair or the use of a small buggy in advance to take them from the check-in desk onto the plane. In these days of increased security awareness it is common sense not to pack anything dangerous, even a kitchen knife, in your hand luggage. Finally, if an item is labelled as 'fragile', it may emerge from a different carousel on arrival.

Confusion: air terminals, especially if unfamiliar or after a long-haul flight, can be very confusing. Age and the inevitable tiredness of travel can make this worse. The crowds, noise, worry about time, managing luggage and getting a good seat all contribute to a sense of unease and confusion. Each little departure from a sense of 'normality' will add to feeling stressed and muddled. Some people like the excitement and rushing about in airports but, for others, the confusing, unrealistic nature can be disturbing.

Case study

John was a frequent flier who spent a total of about four months of the year flying. He considered himself to be an experienced traveller who did not get too stressed. He could not quite work out why he felt worse and just 'out of sorts' in some air terminals and not in others. In fact, he did not like to admit it, but he felt slightly dizzy and could not always remember where he was going at some airports. An older colleague who had flown extensively was sympathetic to John's difficulties and did not in the least think that he was 'just being stupid'. Between the two of them, they worked out that if John sat near a window in the terminal, facing the outside, he felt less intruded on by others and could retain a sense of reality. John also realised that once he was more familiar with the layout of a terminal he then felt more at ease.

In this example John managed to reduce the impact of too many stimuli reaching him by sitting near a window. The noise, public announcements, the feeling of lack of control and impersonality of most air terminals all contribute to a bombardment of unpleasant stimuli. Additionally, many travellers stay 'on alert' in case they miss something, for example, a crucial announcement about their flight. Greater familiarity with flying and with different air terminals will help to reduce the confusion. Even if you are not an experienced traveller, it helps if you know what to expect. So, do not shy away from asking travel agents, family, friends, other experienced travellers and check-in personnel questions. If anxious, make sure you arrive at the airport with a 'to do' list either written down or in your head. Position yourself near an information monitor giving the departure times and the gates if you feel particularly anxious about getting to the departure lounge without rushing. Furthermore, most airports no longer make public announcements over a loud speaker about departure times. Early boarding on the plane also ensures having enough space in the overhead locker to store your hand luggage.

The unfamiliar environment of the air terminal can add extra stress to anyone with sensory or memory impairment. Deterioration of vision, hearing and memory are common to ageing. To minimise confusion:

- if possible, try not to fly alone
- allow plenty of time
- take a break before trying again to get somewhere or trying to do something that feels confusing
- do not hesitate to ask if you get lost or are uncertain about what to do

- do not feel bad about feeling confused: you are not the only person
- remember that the unpleasant feelings of confusion are usually only temporary.

Loss of control: an important element for many people, which underlies their stress at air terminals, is a sense of loss of control. Our luggage quickly disappears on a conveyor belt, we rarely have a choice over seats in the plane, we are herded through passport control, have to suffer the indignities of the security check and may be subjected to impersonal and, at times, discourteous service and be pushed by the crowds. Not surprisingly, many people feel uneasy at this loss of control over their lives and tempers can then flare.

Case study

Ann was a high-powered executive who worked in finance. Before her most recent trip to the USA she had worked unusually long hours. By the time she reached the check-in desk she was feeling tired, particularly as the journey to the airport had taken longer than usual. She was normally a well organised person who always allowed plenty of time and did not like rushing at the last minute. Although she had prebooked her seat when she checked in, she was told that they had no such booking. She was offered a window seat when she had particularly requested an aisle seat. Even though the airline clerk tried to be helpful, Ann felt herself getting more and more angry. The final straw came when the man in the queue behind her accidentally hit her legs with his luggage trolley. She told him in no uncertain terms how clumsy he was. She just managed to stop herself from having an all-out quarrel with him but felt quite shaken by the episode.

Although a certain amount of vigilance is useful in any strange environment, it is not usually possible to control all aspects of the flying experience, however vigilant you are. Stress can be reduced by asking yourself which aspects are within your control and which are not; you can then try to let go of the idea of controlling the things that are out of your control, such as the weather or airport strikes or delays. Delays can be used as an opportunity to catch up on reading, letter writing or making phone calls. If you wish to make a complaint about some aspect of service which you thought that you had under control, as in Ann's example, then make sure that you complain effectively and do not vent your annoyance on someone who has no power to effect any change. It is usually more effective to complain to the airline and not to the hapless desk clerk in front of you. In addition, if you do make a complaint, try to work out beforehand what result you would like from the complaint. Is it an apology or compensation?

Shopping: although for most travellers, shopping at air terminals is both fun and passes the time, thereby reducing boredom, it can sometimes be a compulsive activity. Some people seem to feel compelled to spend money. Foreign currency often does not feel like 'real' money and so is easier to part with. Impulsive purchases can be regretted later on, and can sometimes provoke difficulties between a couple. Furthermore, if the shopping is a response to the stress experienced in air terminals, then spending does not always resolve the stress.

Greater awareness of the sources of your stress can help you to alleviate it in many more ways than just shopping impulsively. Decide if you do want to shop and, if so, what you want to buy. It may be useful to decide on a spending limit before entering the shops. They are there to entice us to spend as much as possible! Avoid rushing into the first shop, just pause and walk round first as that will help you get your bearings.

Stress at air terminals is both a common and normal experience. However stressful it is, remember that it is only temporary and understanding the cause of your particular experience of stress is the first step in trying to reduce it. Some features of air terminal activities are beyond our control. Learning what you can and what you cannot control can often lower your emotional temperature. The points above are not exhaustive but they might help you to compile your own individual strategy list.

5
Coping with jet lag

The term jet lag, technically called circadian desynchronisation, is now commonly used to describe the disruption that occurs to sleep patterns when travelling on long-haul flights. Air travel can produce a wide range of discomforts that may be physical or psychological in nature, or both. To the seasoned traveller, these discomforts may be a familiar inconvenience, while for the uninitiated, they can be an unpleasant surprise. Of all the problems that are associated with long distance air travel, jet lag is possibly the most distressing and unwelcome, as it does not disappear on arrival. Indeed, it may take some days to recover from jet lag and, in certain cases, up to two weeks. The effects may prevent you from enjoying the start of a holiday, getting down to planned business, or adjusting to your regular routine upon your return from a trip abroad. This chapter provides you with some helpful tips on how to anticipate the effects of jet lag, how to cope with and adjust to the symptoms, and how to reduce their impact.

Coping with long distance air travel can be demanding enough, but jet lag may be the last straw for some people and put them off their trip altogether. Even if you manage the effects of jet lag, having your partner or children out of synchronisation in their sleep pattern might prove equally disruptive. However, jet lag is a complex problem and is more than over-tiredness from a long flight or an unwelcome change to your normal sleep cycle. It can affect your mood, motivation, behaviour and performance. It is helpful to have some understanding about what happens to our body when we fly.

The body has a 24-hour 'internal clock' which is sensitive to the urge to eat and sleep, and so on. When we travel across time zones, that is from east to west, or vice versa, the internal clock is out of step with what is happening around us. We may feel hungry at odd times such as the middle of the night or late morning, and be wide awake when everyone around us is preparing to go to bed. These physical sensations may feel worse because we may also be a little anxious or depressed that our normal routine has been disrupted and we feel 'out of synch' with those around us. Unfortunately, our body clock is not as easily re-set as a wrist watch that has lost a few hours or minutes. Adjustment may be slow and habits, such as when we like to eat and sleep, may take several days to settle down. That is assuming that no more travel is likely to occur in the time that we are adjusting to the new time zone. Symptoms of jet lag include:

- extreme fatigue, insomnia or lethargy
- loss of appetite, low energy
- inability to perform well mentally or physically
- constipation
- nausea, aches, pains
- depression, irritability
- disorientation, impaired co-ordination, distortion of time
- poor concentration
- fear
- memory loss
- headache
- loss of sexual interest.

The body clock is, however, more complex than our habits and the urges to eat and sleep. The cycles or internal rhythms are regulated by the release of hormones into the blood supply and include a hormone to lower the body's temperature in preparation for sleep. Body temperature starts falling at around midnight and its lowest level is usually reached at about 4 am. It then rises again at around 10.00 am and remains reasonably constant for the rest of the day. Changes in body temperature are one of the rhythmical patterns we experience. Additionally, our blood pressure falls at night, we use less oxygen and other body parts rest.

We all know that the cues and events that go on around us also affect our habits and routines and are affected by our surroundings such as light/dark – day/night, the availability of food, social and work demands, as well as periods of activity and inactivity. People differ in their responses to these. Some of us are 'night owls' and enjoy working or socialising well into the early hours, while others feel ready for bed not long after dinner and a glass of wine. Infants and some young children may be an anomaly as their 24-hour cycles appear to be compressed into 6–12 hour mini-cycles, and we find ourselves constantly attending to their need to eat or sleep. Somehow, few of us enjoy that routine and bringing up young children may make some of us feel as if we are in a constant state of jet lag.

The 24-hour body clock (or more accurately, 25-hour one to which we make minor adjustments), and the effect of light and darkness, are the main determinants of the rhythms to which we are accustomed. If we change time zones, we disrupt these rhythms, though the effect differs between people. Severity of jet lag is determined by the following:

- age (the older we are, the worse it feels)
- number of time zones crossed

- easterly (versus westerly) direction of travel
- length of the flight
- time of day (or night) the plane arrives
- gender (women may suffer more than men)
- sensitivity to environmental cues (eg. light/dark or people getting ready to eat)
- level of fatigue before travel
- class of travel (greater comfort may reduce the effect and severity of symptoms)
- your mood
- aircraft type (which may determine cabin conditions, length of flight, frequency of air recycling)
- purpose of travel
- seasons
- accumulation of jet lag.

The symptoms of jet lag are usually worse when travelling east than west because most of us can accommodate the occasional 'long day' or 'heavy night'. If you fly from London to New York, you gain five hours, thereby extending the length of your day. Coupled with the fact that you will probably have been seated and relatively inactive for the duration of the seven-hour flight, you may initially find that you have a surge of energy when you get off the plane. However, you may also find that you tire quite easily and need an earlier bedtime than 'usual'. In fact, if you got to bed at 11.00 pm in New York on your day of arrival, your body would really be coping with the effects of a late night since it would feel as if it were four in the morning.

The return journey is likely to prove more stressful in terms of jet lag. The day is significantly shorter when travel is in an easterly direction. Your watch will show 11.00 pm when you arrive back in London, when your body thinks it is still only 6.00 pm. Do not be surprised if you indulge in a midnight snack or have the urge to read or watch TV when everyone else is apparently fast asleep. This can be especially grim and unwelcome if you have just arrived in Singapore or Sydney from London. As much as you have been looking forward to a restful holiday, the reality, for the first few days at least, could be very different. You may feel physically and emotionally drained. This has consequences for your relationships with friends, family or business associates. You can either choose to ignore the effects of jet lag altogether or you can try to cope with or prevent some of the symptoms.

Case study

Rob, aged 26, was invited to speak at his first conference in Dallas, Texas. He was both excited and nervous, and hoped to make a good impression. As he was not a very experienced traveller, he was unaware of the measures he might take to reduce the effects of jet lag. On board the flight from London, he drank a gin and tonic and also managed to consume three small bottles of wine with his meal. This was his first trip in business class and he was keen to enjoy the privilege. On arrival, he caught the bus to the university campus. Although in high spirits, by the time he arrived he was beginning to feel tired and nauseated. His hosts had gone out of their way to give him a grand welcome in true Texas style and a large barbecue was laid on for him. By the early evening he had to excuse himself to go to the toilet where he sat for half an hour feeling unwell. He had the good sense to excuse himself and drank plenty of water before retiring to bed. Rob quickly fell asleep but found himself awake at 4.00am. He felt hung-over and a bit depressed. Although his talk went reasonably well, he was aware that the delivery was not up to his usual high standard. His colleagues still joke about his having had too much to drink and not paying attention to the effects of jet lag.

The rest of this chapter provides hints and tips for overcoming jet lag.

Coping with jet lag

A rule of thumb suggests that it takes the body one full 24-hour cycle to adjust to one new time zone. The trip from London to New York can therefore be expected to take up to five days to fully readjust. This may be unwelcome and pessimistic news, especially if you are going on a short holiday or have an important business meeting. None the less, you can plan your trip and determine how busy and active you will to be, at least in the first few days. It can also benefit the returning traveller who may be keen to extend the trip to the absolute limit, such as going to work directly from the airport after an over-night flight. While many travellers do this, the evidence from research suggests that air travellers should create a buffer for themselves from the effects of jet lag at their destination so that the symptoms recede as soon as possible. In most cases, this entails careful planning about your amount and timing of work, activity, socialising and sleep. Let us look in more detail at how you can cope better with the effects of jet lag.

Adjust your routine before setting out

Some regular air travellers start to prepare for their journey several days before they actually fly. Twenty-four hours before leaving, they set their watch to the new time zone and start to establish new routines around this. You are effectively tricking your body into believing that you are at your destination. Of course, there may be certain limitations to this because you cannot go to sleep on the floor at the office simply because you have decided to adjust your sleeping pattern in preparation for the trip. However, your mind and body will at least be primed for some of the changes that lie ahead. The night before you leave, go to bed as close as possible to the bedtime at your destination and similarly try to wake up (or at least stay in bed) at the waking time of your destination. Light and dark are especially important prompts or cues. Ensure that your bedroom is darkened if you are trying to sleep. If this is not possible, consider using the eyeshades given to passengers on board long-haul flights.

Adjust your routine on the plane

Your internal body clock can also be adjusted once you board the plane. Unfortunately, airline schedules and meal times sometimes go against this so try to choose flights that better suit your departure and arrival times and be prepared to forgo some meals served on board aircraft. What you eat and drink on board the plane may also affect jet lag, and some helpful tips are presented later in this section. As soon as you have completed boarding and located your seat, fasten your safety belt and then set your watch to the local time at your destination. Think of this as a psychological prompt designed to readjust your biological cycles. It follows that you should try to make your sleep cycles fit with those at your destination. If you expect to land early in the morning, then you should try to sleep as much as possible on the flight. If you arrive in the evening, try to stay awake (read, watch the in-flight movie, work) for the duration of the flight and save your sleep until after you have arrived at your destination. Invoke images in your mind of what you are likely to be doing when you reach your destination. If you arrive in the morning, imagine yourself having a long and busy day ahead. If it is an evening arrival, think about the shower and bed that await you. The following days should also be planned accordingly. Most people find that they have more energy in the evening if they have travelled from west to east, while those who have flown from east to west generally find that their energy levels peak in the morning.

Change your sleep patterns

Everyone has, at some point, had difficulty sleeping. Perhaps work stress or relationship problems disrupted normal sleep patterns. The opposite is also sometimes true, that we have the need or urge to sleep more than usual. Boredom, a period of stress or simply feeling relaxed can cause this. Happily, sleep problems can usually be remedied and new patterns can be established (see *Chapter 3*). This is good news for the air traveller with jet lag who either needs to establish a new sleep routine or cope with a disrupted one. The first step in changing any sleep pattern is to try to sleep at night — it makes sense in terms of your social and physical needs. Delaying sleep or ignoring the local rhythm will only drive the effects of jet lag deeper. Whether on board a plane, or at your destination, the following suggestions can help to induce sleep:

• Think about the rituals you normally follow when you go to sleep (eg. do you brush your teeth first, have a glass of warm milk, read a little) and try to follow these. Sleep sometimes comes more easily after eating a meal, but opt for a light meal

- Create conditions around you which are likely to facilitate sleep (cover yourself with a blanket; switch off the radio or TV; lie back as best possible) and ensure that you are comfortable

- Loosen clothing if you are sitting on a plane (such as a belt or tie and perhaps take off your shoes)

- Reduce noise levels by using ear plugs

- Cover your eyes using an eye shade if there is too much light

- Get rid of any worries from your mind. You can think about your work or any social demands at another time

- Breathe deeply and slowly

- Remember that even if you are unable to sleep, you may be able to rest or nap

- Sleeping pills may help to induce sleep. It is best to take a short-acting pill to avoid the 'hangover' effect that sometimes accompanies some sleeping pills and which may make jet lag feel worse. Avoid taking a pill until you are at least half an hour into a flight. You may find sleep comes more easily once the departure and take off has been completed. Also, if there is a delay on the ground, you may find yourself asleep at a time when you need to be alert

- The sleep hormone, melatonin, is a popular alternative to sleeping pills and is available in the United States and on private prescription in the UK. Taking this nocturnal hormone before going to sleep can help to re-set the body clock.

Respond to social and physical cues

Bright light helps to resynchronise your body clock. Sunlight is especially effective and you should aim to spend as much time as possible outdoors at your destination. Exposure to a bright, artificial light can also help. Some regular fliers have told us that taking a long hot bath as soon as possible at their destination is both relaxing and helps to re-set the body clock. Aromatherapy, massage and simple relaxation exercises can also help. Travelling in a group, rather than alone, has been found to act as a buffer against some of the symptoms of jet lag; it may be that those who travel alone do not have the social support and motivation of the group and have more stress to contend with when they travel. Self-talk can also help. Motivate yourself to be alert or to relax. Invoke images in your mind of yourself being active or relaxed. The mind and body are, after all, connected and thinking can change our feelings and behaviour, while doing things differently in turn alters our thoughts and ideas.

Be more attentive to what and when you eat

Meal times and food intake can affect jet lag. Anticipation is often high regarding airline meals yet the reality is that they often lack wholesome complex carbohydrates and may be high in levels of sugar, fat and salt. Most meals are prepared long before the flight, chilled and then re-heated on board the plane in convection ovens. Taste is sometimes compromised, both as a result of this process and the inefficiency of our taste buds in the dry, low pressure cabin environment. Furthermore, our stomach and intestines tend to swell up at altitude and a high protein meal does little to settle this. Worse still, meal times on board planes often reflect the airline's desire to feed people as soon as possible so that the crew can get on with other tasks or rest, rather than being synchronised with the local time of either the destination or point of departure. The advice from nutritionists and frequent fliers is as follow:

- opt for simple, high carbohydrate meals (avoid too much meat and rich sauces)
- fruit and vegetables are a good option
- take your own food on the plane if you are concerned that the choice of meal will be limited and less healthy; it also allows you to eat when you need to in order to re-synchronise your body clock
- eat a light meal; after all, you are likely to be fairly inactive for the duration of the flight
- some people try to 're-set' their digestive body clock by fasting and abstaining from solid food while travelling. However, remember to keep up your fluid intake
- eat when you feel hungry rather than when food is put in front of you
- avoid alcohol, tea, coffee and fizzy drinks due to dehydration, bloating and the increased urge to go to the toilet. Still water or fruit drinks are preferable
- a high protein meal or snack on arrival will help to boost your energy levels
- some air travellers find that fresh carrot juice taken after the flight helps counter some of the effects of jet lag.

Undertake light exercise

Long periods of inactivity and being confined to one's seat on a plane are not conducive to one's physical and psychological well-being. However, air travellers start their journey with a fair bit of aerobic activity – hauling luggage, walking through air terminals, and sometimes sprinting to the departure gate. Many passengers complain of stiff muscles and general bodily aches and pains when they have jet lag. 'Economy class syndrome' was coined by doctors who found that some passengers were more at risk of blood clots on board planes and many complained that blood pooled around their ankles, sometimes making walking uncomfortable.

While in your seat you should practice some stretching exercises and undertake light exercise from time to time. However, always consult your doctor first. Rotate your ankles, stretch your arms and legs, pull in your stomach and rotate your shoulders. Where permitted, you can also walk around the plane and do a few squats. These exercises will help keep the blood circulating, reduce fatigue and increase alertness for when you arrive.

Jet lag is at best unpleasant and at worse debilitating. It affects you at a time when you should be looking forward to recovering from the flight. Air travellers can help themselves to reduce the effects of jet lag and cope better with some of the unpleasant symptoms. These steps, that can be taken to address jet lag before, during and after the flight, should also impress upon the reader that you can positively influence your physical and psychological experience of the journey by anticipating and addressing the effects of jet lag. You can also control some aspects of flying and ensure that the experience is more positive.

6
The effect of air travel on relationships

Travel nearly always affects relationships, whether or not you travel with someone. There is a myth that the enjoyment of travel is enhanced by flying with a friend or partner. There is another popular myth that relationship problems can be solved or smoothed over by travel. By way of contrast, some people do not always consider the effect of their travels on their relationships nor on those left at home. This chapter considers some of the effects of plane journeys on families and couples and suggests strategies to cope with these effects.

Escaping from relationship difficulties by travelling

Relationships are inevitably affected by travel, irrespective of the purpose of the trip. For some, the effect on relationships may be positive, while for others it further aggravates an already troubled relationship. It is not really known how often journeys are undertaken to escape from relationship difficulties. Some business trips seem like a good idea because they combine business with an escape from routine, boredom or tension between partners at home. Widely publicised data informs us that marriages and couple relationships are breaking down with increasing frequency. One in three first marriages in the United Kingdom ends in divorce, and the figure is even higher for second marriages. Indeed, most of us have some kind of personal experience, even if it is indirect, of a relationship in jeopardy.

A typical scenario depicts one partner, usually the woman, reporting that there is not enough quality time devoted to their relationship. Where the husband is the main breadwinner, complaints sometimes surface that **he** is away too much and that **she** comes second to his business. In turn, **he** argues that **she** does not appreciate what he does for her by working so hard. The solution for some couples is to spend more time together. For others, the time spent apart can actually lead to more intense excitement when they are together, provided they mutually feel secure about the other's commitment and understanding about fidelity.

Case study

Sarah and John are considered by their friends 'to have it all'. They are an attractive successful couple in their thirties, with two sons aged four and two. John is the financial director of a medium-sized company and travels extensively on business to the Far East. His business necessitates monthly flights to attend meetings. Sarah gave up her job as a personnel manager after the birth of their first son. She misses the excitement of her job but feels that it important to stay at home at least until both boys are at school. Although she supports John's ambition to climb rapidly up the company ladder, she increasingly feels left out of his life. Whereas in the past they would spend hours together talking about his business, more often than not he now says that he is too tired to talk after all the stress and hassles of travelling and, consequently, Sarah feels both upset and angry. She does consider that her wish for more intimacy is at times unreasonable, given how tired John seems to be after each trip, but she also feels that, unless there is more closeness, their marriage could be at risk. She has started to ask herself whether John might be having an affair as he seems to be so uninterested in her. John, for his part, both looks forward to his trips away but also feels guilty about being away so much, especially with the boys making so many demands on Sarah. He loves the excitement of flying although he finds it exhausting and stressful, particularly if there are deadlines to meet and he gets delayed. He likes to use his frequent flier miles as a perk for the occasional trip with the family. However, he dislikes Sarah's nagging as soon as he gets home and recently he has started to add on an extra day to some of his business trips. He tells himself that he needs to unwind before he can re-enter the home environment.

The example of John and Sarah illustrates the potential for erosion in a marriage caused, in part, by the frequent absences. It also highlights the risk of simply taking the commonly given advice to couples to 'take a holiday together' to repair a potentially unstable relationship. This advice can be helpful if it leads to improved communication and increased intimacy, but often the result can lead to a fracturing of the relationship as pent-up resentments are voiced and mutual non-comprehension escalates the resentments into warfare. Caution is necessary in taking a 'repair' trip if travel is undertaken solely or in part to escape from relationship difficulties.

Relationship questions

Here are some questions that might be useful for you to consider, particularly if the example of John and Sarah is 'close to home'. Think about your responses and then try to imagine what your partner's views might be. You might even find the opportunity and courage to discuss these openly at home.

1. How essential to your work is travel?

2. How essential to your work is this particular journey?

3. If you decided not to fly, what might be the consequences to your job?

4. If you did fly what might be the difficulties or consequences for your partner?

5. Is there a sense of your trying to escape from your home situation? If so, what precisely are you escaping from?

6. How well do you communicate the need to travel with your partner?

7. How is your partner included in your travel plans?

8. What happens at home while you are away?

9. What might happen if the 'buzz' goes out of your relationship?

Even if a couple agree that flying by one partner is necessary and poses no risks to the relationship, it is probably a good idea to check from time to time that this still holds true. After all, the stress associated with travel and the repercussions for relationships are cumulative. What works at one point in a couple's relationship may not do so several years down the road when relationship and family circumstances may have changed. Ken and Linda illustrate this dilemma.

Case study

They have lived together for eleven years since they met in their second year at university. Ken is a successful journalist who travels around the world reporting from war zones. Linda is a research scientist who works in the pharmaceutical industry. They regard themselves as an ambitious dual-career couple who are committed to each other, although they lead largely independent lives. In practice, this has often resulted in Ken not telling Linda when or where he was travelling. Similarly, if Linda had to work late at the lab, she did not let Ken know. This arrangement worked well for both of them for several years. They were deeply interested in what the other had been doing during the time apart and sex was great. But their mutual satisfaction changed after the birth of their first baby, even though both had wanted to have a child. They hoped that with sufficient organisation nothing much would have to change in their exciting lives. But Linda, who was the primary caretaker of their son, Tom, found herself resenting not only Ken's frequent absences but also his lack of consideration in not telling her when he was going to be away. Ken did not realise the extent of Linda's resentment. It was Ken's mother who brought matters out into the open when she innocently asked Ken, in front of Linda, when was his next trip and that he must make sure that he was home for Tom's first birthday. Linda burst into tears and rushed out of the room. Ken went after her and they ended up talking far into the night. Linda was able to tell Ken that she felt alone and unsupported, and Ken could empathise with her feelings. He agreed to give Linda his timetable and try to stay at home more. They agreed that they would try to find a mother's help, rather than rely on their hit-and-miss arrangement with Linda's mother, so that Linda had more time for her work. They also resolved to tell each other if either felt unhappy with the new arrangement and not to let resentments build up.

Escaping from relationship difficulties; the partner left behind

Ken and Linda's story illustrates the need to renegotiate the 'rules' and conditions of a partnership, particularly at crucial points in the development of the relationship. Increasing emotional distance between a couple can lead to decreasing intimacy. More relationships end because of indifference and lack of interest in each other than because of fights and quarrels. Pilots, airline employees, business people, journalists, media artists, military personnel and others whose occupations may involve frequent travel are particularly at risk. However, researchers are sometimes more interested in the plight of the person travelling and his/her stress than in the person who remains at home. Evidence suggests that divorce rates are higher among couples who are often parted. Also, geographical distance is cited as the most common reason for friendships ending, especially between men. Women have an advantage over men and seem better able to sustain friendships with other women despite distance: these friendships can be supportive and, indeed, help them to sustain more intimate relationships.

The intermittent spouse syndrome

Separation from one's spouse, friends, home and family is a significant contributing factor to travel stress, both for the person travelling and the person at home. Psychologists have recognised that certain patterns emerge and are repeated in relationships where one or both partners are frequent travellers.

These patterns have been collectively termed the 'Intermittent Spouse Syndrome'and include some of the following.

Pre-flight tensions

Although the tensions for the traveller and his or her spouse may be experienced differently, the underlying anxiety or unhappiness is usually the result of the fear of separation. Geographical separation from family, friends and familiar surroundings can lead to a loss of psychological well-being and stability. This feeling, induced by impending separation, can lead to tensions, both within the individual and between the couple, resulting in quarrels or withdrawal. Frequent absences can erode the sense of belonging to family, friends or neighbourhood and lead to prolonged feelings of alienation. For the person travelling, the pre-flight tensions may involve such issues as the need to organise a business meeting with unknown colleagues in another country, potential business conflicts during absences, flight scheduling difficulties, as well as worrying about how the family will cope during his or her absence. Men are especially susceptible to the effects of these tensions because research demonstrates that they may avoid sharing their worries with their spouse; particularly sharing what they see as the 'trivial' incidents or worries of the day.

During travel

The person left behind often reacts in one of the following ways:
- With feelings of abandonment and insecurity leading, at times, to depression or anxiety. For example, ' I feel as if I am

a one-parent family and I have sole responsibility for everything while he is away and then, when he returns, he is too tired to do anything'.

- With mixed feelings of relief and loneliness. For example, 'Although I feel lonely when he is away, at least I can get on with my interests without having to consider his needs'.
- With relief. For example, 'There is so much tension in the house that I breathe a huge sigh of relief every time he leaves'.

Maintaining relationships, even from a distance, can reduce the detrimental effects of travel both on the traveller and the partner left behind. Modern methods of communication can be used not only to relay information and recount daily events, but also to share feelings about those events. Letters, telephones, faxes and e-mails can all be used not only to impart information but also to share and inquire about feelings with friends and family.

On the return

Integration back into the home for the 'intermittent spouse' can pose difficulties both for the returning spouse/partner and the person left at home. Misunderstandings commonly arise from different, and unspoken, expectations. The spouse left behind may wish her husband to immediately take up the threads of home life. After all, she may have had to cope with the house, children and her job and may want to be able to share some of the burdens and joys experienced during his absence. On the other hand, the partner may be jet lagged and exhausted and have no inclination to engage in lively conversation, sorting out problems with children, elderly parents or the bank. Time to unwind, with no pressures on either side, can help re-entry for both partners. It helps to have some 'protected' couple time together, without children or family. But the 'protected' couple time should not be spent reiterating problems to each other — it is important to have some fun too. With the huge increase in the number of people who travel by air, many more couples are likely to experience some variant of 'the intermittent spouse syndrome'. The homecoming is often the most difficult part of travelling, particularly if there are unreasonably high expectations of romance and intimacy. If a couple have different expectations, then disappointment may ensue, putting a further strain on the relationship. If intimacy is affected as a result of frequent absences then there may be a risk of an extramarital relationship. The frequent flier may discover that his wife or partner has been having an affair during his absence, or that she wants to end their marriage because of his absences or, it may be that her feelings about his flying may be just the tip of the relationship iceberg. He, too, may look to others for sexual and relationship gratification, either while abroad or on his return. If the couple cannot discover a way to address their difficulties, then the next journey should probably be in the direction of the nearest Relate counsellor or marital therapist.

Strategies to help you cope with the 'intermittent spouse syndrome' include:

- anticipate the process and pressures before they occur and discuss them together
- keep in touch while apart, even just to say 'Hello' or 'I am thinking of you'
- lower your expectations at times of emotional intensity, such as separation or homecoming
- allow time for a gradual emotional re-entry back into the family and couple.

Together on the flight

Couples who enjoy a secure relationship can generally manage adversity well and this includes the stress of flying. However, for a significant number of couples the stress of air travel can highlight a difficulty in their relationship which can turn a difficult flight into a nightmare. By breaking down the component parts of the flight, and the difficulties faced by the couple, they can be helped to manage each in turn. The following provides a template for this.

Purpose of flight

What is the purpose of the flight for you and your partner ? Is it:
- a routine holiday
- a special holiday (an anniversary/birthday surprise)
- a business trip for one or both of you
- a combination of business and holiday
- a once in a lifetime long-haul flight to an exotic destination.

What are your expectations of the flight?
- to have fun
- a necessary and boring part of business life
- an opportunity to catch up on reading/paperwork/thinking/planning
- a chance to make new friends
- a setting for relaxation and letting go
- just the fastest means of getting from A to B
- start of a cure for relationship problems.

Once you have clarified the purpose of your flight and your

expectations, you are less likely to be disappointed or, indeed, try to solve a difficulty with the 'wrong' solution.

Case study

For John and Sarah the flight to Los Angeles had a different meaning. For John it was an opportunity to combine a business trip with a few days (just three days in his mind) with Sarah. He was only half looking forward to the few days with Sarah although he hoped that they could be more relaxed with each other. For Sarah, however, it was an opportunity to have John's undivided attention. She felt apprehensive about flying but was looking forward to a whole week together after his business was completed. In anticipation, she bought herself some sexy new underwear and invested in a new and expensive haircut.

Pre-flight arrangements

If there are tensions between a couple, then even the most routine pre-flight decisions can become snarled. For John and Sarah, their pre-flight arrangements did not even start from the same base.

Each had different expectations of the trip, as well as different expectations as to who was taking on which tasks. John expected Sarah to book the flights, whereas Sarah hoped that John was going to surprise her with a business class ticket and a stay in a romantic hotel following his business meetings. Matters came to a head ten days before they were due to leave when John casually asked Sarah how the arrangements were coming along as he needed an exact itinerary. The argument became heated as each blamed the other for not 'getting their act together'. John said that he did not have the time to take more than two days after his business meetings for a holiday and did she really mean to travel with him with such a ridiculous haircut! She burst into tears and said that he never considered her feelings or needs.

The example of John and Sarah highlights the spill-over from relationship difficulties to other arenas that then become problematic. A contrasting story is that of Dave and Jill.

Case study

Dave and Jill had been married for thirty years. They had three grown-up children and four grandchildren. Dave had recently been made redundant from his job as a car salesman and he and Jill had decided to use some of his redundancy money to go on the holiday of a lifetime. They spent hours together pouring over holiday brochures. Jill fancied a game park trip to Africa, whereas Dave preferred a deep sea diving adventure holiday, but they each compromised and felt satisfied with their solutions. They would go to Australia where Dave could dive, and then they would both explore the rain forests of Australia and look at the wild life. They worked out how to divide up the tasks involved and got on with them. For them, part of the excitement lay in the joint planning.

At the airport

The general issues about airport stress have been described in *Chapter 4*. This section deals with the effect of airport stress on couples. As has already been described, individuals respond differently to the stress of airports and, for couples, the cumulative stress of their individual tensions can be considerable. Who has not witnessed a tired, harassed-looking couple rushing up to the check-in counter still quarrelling about whose fault it is that they were cutting it so fine, had left the suitcase key behind and forgotten about the cat? This same couple may go on to argue about who has the window seat on the plane and who had forgotten to order their vegetarian meal, though both may feel aggrieved that it is a non-smoking flight.

By the time Sarah and John reached the airport they could only just manage to be polite to each other. Their journey was made even more stressful by the traffic jams they encountered, then there was a long wait for the air terminal bus after parking their car. In the preparations, both practical and emotional for this trip, Sarah managed not to think about the usual worries that plague her on any flight but, in the departure lounge, she began to feel slightly shakey, a bit sweaty, and was aware that her heart was beating very fast. She did not want to tell John as she feared that he would just tell her to keep calm. She envied the ease with which he sailed through all the fuss and bother of the check-in, security, the duty-free shop. She decided that a drink would calm her down, so she crept off to the Bar and drank three quick martinis before re-joining John. Meanwhile John noticed how pale Sarah looked but did not say anything to her about her pallor; he thought that if he did she would start to complain about everything being wrong, from the seats they were allocated, to the crowds in the departure lounge. He would then feel even more annoyed with her. He would also feel useless because he never knew what to do when Sarah went white as a sheet and started to hyperventilate.

Sarah exhibits some of the common physical and emotional symptoms of anxiety brought on by the stress and apprehension associated with flying. Her solution of drinking alcohol to relax is one used by at least a third of those who experience anxiety when travelling and, like many other fearful travellers, she does not communicate her distress or seek any professional help for her fear. Furthermore, she is trying to deal with a relationship problem by going away with her husband, but he is the last person she wants to talk to about her symptoms. This combination of uncertainty in her personal life and air travel stress has not only led Sarah to use alcohol, but has also resulted in confused feelings and behaviour.

Strategies for a couple to deal with air travel anxiety

Prevention: *Chapter 3* offers suggestions of strategies and self-help ideas to overcome fears associated with flying that can both prevent and treat anxiety. It usually helps the anxious person if their partner knows about their flying anxieties and knows how to help. An important aspect of prevention is know-ledge. Fear of flying is not the result of weakness or stupidity.

Be specific about your worries: The anxious individual should preferably tell their partner about their travel and relationship worries long before starting out on the journey to the airport. If there is tension between a couple then it is very important to be specific. For example; 'I worry about getting in the way and then your getting cross with me', rather than saying, ' I hope we can stay calm as airports make me feel dizzy and I will want to sit down as soon as possible, and you might shout at me and lose your temper just like you did last year at Athens Airport'.

Clarity: Try to work out what you would like your partner to do in the event of increasing tension between you. For example, 'Let us stay calm whatever happens, rather than trying to work out what is wrong at a time of intense feelings'.

Be allies: Work together to conquer relationship difficulties. This can greatly diminish their impact on the couple.

No blame: Blame between a couple is counter-productive. Even if you consider the other person as primarily responsible for the difficulties between you, it is usually not helpful to say so. Blame usually leads to counter-accusations and increasing tension. It also gets in the way of dealing with the problem.

No shame: Try not to embarrass or shame each other, especially in front of other people. In stressful conditions, such as airports, it is often better to hold one's tongue than to lash out and later regret it.

On the flight

Couples flying together have to contend with their own individual reactions to the flight as well as those of their partner. One partner's flying stress is likely to be exacerbated in the presence of couple relationship problems. Similarly, couple difficulties make it more difficult to address or ameliorate an individual's flight fears.

Sarah was feeling light-headed by the time she and John finally reached their seat on the plane. Sarah insisted on sitting in the aisle seat which left John cramped in the middle seat between Sarah and a large man at the window seat. Sarah preferred the aisle seat as she would feel less claustrophobic and it was easier to get to the toilet from an aisle seat. John would have preferred the window seat as he liked to look out of the window — he never ceased to be amazed at the beauty of the clouds and the view of mountains. He apologetically told the flight attendant that his wife was an anxious traveller but Sarah would have preferred him not to say anything as she did not want to draw attention to herself. On sitting down she hissed loudly at him, 'Why did you have to say anything? I will be perfectly all right just as long as I don't faint or am sick'. As there is no privacy in a cabin, the teenager in the row in front turned round, on hearing Sarah, and said to his girl friend, 'Just our luck to sit near some stupid woman who will puke'.

The enclosed atmosphere inside the plane can add a sense of theatre to even the most ordinary exchanges between a couple. Even though flying may be a familiar experience for many, it can still impart a sense of the dramatic. The closing of the doors and the muted instructions to the crew before take-off seem like the prelude to a play where passengers are both onlookers and participants. That prelude can herald the start of anxiety for nervous passengers or an increase in symptoms in the already worried fliers. There is no escape from the developing drama; unlike the theatre one cannot just leave if one does not like the performance. People react differently to any disturbance between a couple in the air. Some are fascinated and feel as if they are watching a gradually unfolding performance. What will happen next? By contrast, others are made to feel very uncomfortable by the intrusion into their 'space' of unwanted conversation. A sense of discomfort may also result from 'taking sides' with one of the quarrelling pair or hearing one's own secret worries spoken out loud.

Making new relationships on a plane

People sometimes say things to their partners or, indeed, to absolute strangers on board a plane that they would never dream of saying on the ground. The strange and unfamiliar environment fosters an atmosphere of the confessional. A commonly reported experience is that of someone telling the person in the adjacent seat all manner of deeply personal stories about themselves; the rationale given by the person recounting their story is usually along the lines of, 'Well, I will never see you again; you seemed to be sympathetic and I needed to talk through my problem'. Or, 'I feel more courageous and I just like the look of you so I will say something'. Although rarely put into words, it appears as if passengers feel less constrained by the everyday rules which usually govern what we say to strangers. People engage in a life review as thoughts of mortality and being in the air gives a chance to review and have a different perspective on life. Confessing or just talking to one's neighbour on a plane can be beneficial for both parties. It provides interest on long-haul flights, is a useful distraction from anxiety, can result in illuminating ideas and be fun, and can sometimes result in forming new and lasting relationships. However, once inside the air terminal it is as if these 'intimate' conversations never took place. At the luggage carousel few people seem to continue their conversations any further.

However, for some, attempted conversations can be an unwelcome intrusion. Strategies to prevent such intrusion include the following: look engrossed in a book, do not maintain any eye contact, give monosyllabic replies, keep on your headphones; and, if all else fails, pretend not to speak the same language as the intruder.

Mood difficulties and flying

Even if a couple holiday together, not necessarily because they have to repair their relationship, care is required if there are pre-existing mood difficulties as illustrated by the example below.

Case study

Peter and Sue had decided to fly off to the sunshine to beat Peter's winter 'blues'. It was their first winter together as a couple since Peter's divorce from Anne seven months previously. (Anne had wanted to divorce Peter more than three years ago while Peter was trying to save his marriage.) He had met Sue at a singles club soon after his divorce and they started to live together shortly afterwards. Sue knew that Peter had always felt a bit low as the winter nights grew longer and she wanted their first winter living together to be memorable, as she still felt the shadow of Anne cast gloom on their relationship. For his part, Peter desperately wanted everything to work out with Sue and readily agreed to go away with her. He was grateful that she seemed so understanding of his low mood, although he did at times feel a bit like a small boy who needed looking after by his 'mum'. In order to bolster his self-esteem he accepted the drinks on offer as soon as the flight attendant brought round the trolley. Sue watched with some alarm as the more Peter drank the more depressed he seemed to become and eventually he started to weep uncontrollably. As Sue tried desperately to calm him down, he just went on and on about being a loser, a lousy husband and that he would be better off dead and how could any woman want him.

It is well documented that an overload of life events can precipitate a depressive illness in vulnerable people. Furthermore, some depressed people may not cope well with rapid social and environmental changes. In this example, Peter, already prone to low moods, was having to cope with two important life events; namely, his recent divorce and the start of a new relationship. Also, he was flying east to west, which has been shown to correlate with a significant increase in the incidence of depression in predisposed individuals. Excessive alcohol intake in depressed people usually makes the depression worse, although it is commonly used to try to cope with the symptoms of depression. For her part, Sue was at her wits end and the more she worried about Peter, the shriller and louder her voice became. If depressed (or with a tendency towards depression):

- limit the length of the flight, especially east to west (as vulnerable people tend to become more depressed when flying from east to west)
- think about postponing the flight if you or you partner have had more than two serious life events in the past year, (eg. death, divorce, illness, moving house)
- discuss taking a course of antidepressant medication with your GP at least two weeks before flying; (many antidepressants take at least two weeks to have any effect)
- restrict your alcohol intake, especially if taking antidepressants, as the effects of alcohol and anti-depressants are additive and can lead to extremes of tiredness or emotional instability
- have your in-depth conversations about relation-ships before the flight
- work out with your partner what would be helpful in the event of becoming more depressed before leaving home

- if you are trying to reassure your depressed partner on a flight, do not raise your voice and try to stay calm. Speak in short clear sentences
- explain to the cabin staff what is happening and ask if it is possible to change your seats to a less crowded part of the plane or ask to sit separately from each other if that would help to calm everything down
- if you feel the need to provide an explanation of either your own or your partner's depressed behaviour to surrounding passengers, just a few sentences on the lines of, 'I/he/she have/has been having a difficult time recently'
- emphasise the positive aspects of the flight, and of your relationship to both yourself and your partner, by talking about what you will do at your destination, especially pleasurable activities and speaking of what works well for you as a couple.

The affair in the air

Much more commonly reported than mood problems are affairs in the air, or the meeting on the plane that results in an affair as a consequence of couple difficulties on the ground.

There is no reliable research into the frequency of flights taken by couples having an extramarital affair, or about the numbers of affairs that start at airports or on planes. For a couple having an affair and not wishing to be discovered, air travel may seem relatively 'safe' — most airports are large and anonymity seems guaranteed. Travel arrangements can usually be made to disguise the affair. Not many people travelling secretly with their secretary are discovered in quite such public circumstances as the Israeli businessman in 1976 whose flight to Paris was highjacked and ended up in Entebbe!

What are the possible, and at this stage tentative, explanations for individuals having an affair in the air?

- individuals may deliberately seek out travel in order to 'invite' an affair as an escape from domestic problems
- travel brings us into contact with a wide range of people with an increased risk/chance of this happening
- travel is a great leveller and, as a result, bored, frustrated or vulnerable people may seek reassurance from others and become more intimate
- proximity to someone whom you find attractive for hours at a stretch is an ideal setting for the start of an affair
- according to flying folklore, flight attendants offer 'tea/coffee/me', with some airlines playing on this image in their adverts
- anonymity, in which airports and planes provide secure and anonymous settings for affairs.

If the couple having an affair feel themselves to be 'invisible', then they may feel that any sexual activity between them is likewise 'invisible'and behaviour may be less constrained by the 'rules' people more or less follow on the ground. The expectations of the relationship can heighten in the enclosed space of the aircraft cabin and literally shutting out the real world increases their sense of closeness. The stress of the environment can also make this kind of couple relationship more exciting. One possible psychological mechanism for the excitement of affairs starting or continuing in aeroplanes is the unconscious link between the 'risk' of flying and the 'risk' of the affair.

Case study

Sharon and Derek had known each other for about six months and they worked in the same company, Sharon being Derek's immediate boss. Sharon was unhappily married and she had been confiding in Derek about her marital problems. Their conversations had become more and more intimate and for the past two months they had been having an affair. They planned a two-week holiday together in the Caribbean following on from a business meeting. When flying, Sharon was usually bad-tempered and irritable until the plane took of; Derek usually just shut off from his surroundings. However, they both found the flight much more fun this time. They had talked about trying to have sex on the flight and the riskiness of the venture just added spice to their affair. When the lights went off in the cabin, Sharon and Derek found ways of engaging in sexual activity — the risk increased their enjoyment. They knew that they were making a bit of noise but passion made them oblivious to the surrounding passengers.

What if you are sitting in seats close to Sharon and Derek and do not share their sense of enjoyment? As with many kinds of antisocial or disinhibited behaviour, people will bring their own set of beliefs to the activity as well as their own set of circumstances. Those who disapprove of any show of intimacy in public places, and who are also feeling stressed by the flight, are likely to be among those most affected by the kind of scene described above. Their behaviour is contrary to common sense and may indeed infringe the law about behaviour in public places.

Not everyone would share Sharon and Derek's idea of fun and such behaviour would contravene accepted codes of behaviour on a plane and might constitute a nuisance. A man was recently charged for continuing to display pornography on his lap-top computer while in a plane despite being asked to turn it off. If you wish to complain it usually helps to start discretely by letting the couple know that you are 'on to them' by coughing, talking about their behaviour to your neighbour, quietly expressing disapproval or even making fun of them (although at this stage making fun should be undertaken tolerantly or with amusement). Escalating the nature of the complaint can be tried if a softly, softly approach does not work. Then you could call the flight attendant and discretely ask them to handle the problem, put lights on and/or more firmly tell the couple of your discomfort. Loud criticisms hurled at people are rarely effective. A polite but firm request to stop what they are doing because you cannot sleep or read is usually more effective.

This chapter has considered how air travel affects relationships throughout a journey from the planning stage to the return home. In order to reduce the negative impact of plane journeys on relationships you could consider the following:

- difficult couple problems are not usually solved by flying together
- work out rules and roles as a couple before setting out for the airport
- communicate clearly with each other what your needs and expectations are
- be tolerant of your partner's flying problems.

7

Flying with children

In recent years, inclusive package holidays and competitive fare structures have led to an increase in the number of families travelling by air and few parents feel that having children should be an impediment to travel. There is greater experimentation and less rigidity about travelling with children as we live in a much more mobile culture. Indeed, children increasingly travel unaccompanied and some airlines make special provision for this.

Airlines, however, differ greatly in the service they offer to adults travelling with children, although there is a measure of agreement about fare structure. Children under the age of two may pay a small percentage of the full adult fare on some international flights, provided that they are accompanied by a fare-paying adult but this may not entitle them to a seat, a meal or a baggage allowance. Most airlines are, in fact, fairly lenient about the amount of baggage brought on board for infants and toddlers, but it is important to check with the airline on any restrictions they place on the amount of carry-on baggage.

Once the practicalities have been sorted out, it can be fun and add an extra dimension to the journey to fly with children. However, it can also be fraught, both for the children and their parents, as well as for the other passengers and cabin crew and the first section of this chapter explores the emotional and practical aspects of flying with children. There are many good books and articles giving invaluable 'how to' advice on travelling with children but little has been published on the underlying psychology of this method of travelling. However, much is known about children's development, and about how families function when under stress, and these ideas are applied to the particular difficulties encountered when flying with children.

Psychology and flying with children

Attachment and the strange environment

Since the trail-blazing work on human attachment by child psychiatrist and psychoanalyst, Dr John Bowlby, there has been recognition of the harmful effects that separation can have on children's development. In his book, *Separation* (1975), he studied the anxiety produced by separation as well as every day situations that cause fear. He concluded that fear is most often aroused by intrinsically harmless situations which we perceive as warnings of an increased risk of danger. When humans were cave dwellers, it was useful from an evolutionary point of view to feel fear in potentially threatening situations. In situations of potential threat we would naturally seek a secure attachment figure to reassure and protect us from predators. Furthermore, the person in the care-giving role would also respond to the fear or anxiety of the more dependent individual by offering protection. It is not too far-fetched to apply such ideas about attachment and separation to many commonly observed and felt difficulties between parents and children at the airport and on board an aircraft.

Case study

Suzie was flying for the first time, with her six-month-old baby daughter to Italy to join her partner, Andy, who was already there on business. He was due to meet her and their baby,

Laura, at the airport and then they were going to drive to join friends at the seaside. Suzie did not feel very confident about travelling alone with Laura but did not want to make a fuss. She would phone her own mother every day to ask her advice about Laura. She was a difficult baby and would not settle and cried a lot and seemed very 'jumpy' to Suzie. Suzie's mother said that she had been just the same when she was a baby and that she should not fuss so much and just leave Laura alone. This advice, though well intended, just made Suzie feel inadequate. Although she tried to prepare for the flight, and took treble supplies of everything, she still could not calm Laura once they were on board the plane. Laura fretted, worrying Suzie who kept picking her up and putting her down in the carrycot provided by the airline. She was certain that her neighbours were fed up with her and her noisy daughter. Laura seemed to jump every time there was a strange noise in the cabin, she screamed at take-off and landing and was inconsolable. Suzie just prayed that the flight would end soon. She wished that Andy had flown with them.

This is seen as an example of an insecure attachment leading to a baby's fretful behaviour in a strange environment. It is easy to underestimate how disturbing the change of routine and the change of environment can be, even to small babies, and in such conditions it is normal for babies and small children to seek reassurance from their parents. Small babies can only do this by making a fuss or crying or fretting. If the attachment to the caregiver is an anxious one, then it is much harder for the caregiver to give that reassurance. A secure attachment, in which the baby's worries can be attended to by the mother, leads to protection from the anxiety-inducing effects of the outside environment. Having said this, it does not necessarily follow that securely attached children always travel well and individual personality traits are important. An infant's behaviour will be affected by the nature of his or her attachment to the caregiver and also by the composition of the family.

Family composition

We all have ideas about the effect on us of being the first, or second, or third born in a family. There cannot be many of us who have not at some time said, 'It's not fair', on account of a perceived unfairness due to being the youngest, oldest or middle child. Some of us have an idea that being the oldest brings with it extra responsibility and privilege. Parents often say, 'He is anxious because he was our first born'. In other words, certain personality attributes may be attached to birth order. This is not to ignore the importance of gender, culture and personal history in attributing characteristics to our children but family composition is a relevant factor in understanding infant and child behaviour. An understanding of the psychological factors underlying your child's behaviour may help manage your flight stress. It also helps to have 'realistic' expectations of your children on a flight. Encourage the positive aspects of your child's personality and sibling relationship in order to arrive at your destination in good emotional shape. For example, your 10-year-old's 'bossiness' in relation to her fidgety younger brother can be a great asset on a flight but she may need a little coaching not to be too heavy-handed with him.

Case study

Jeremy and Sam were seven and five years old respectively and were travelling with their parents, Pat and Simon, on a package holiday to France. Pat had packed extra toys for each boy and she gave them these little treats at well-spaced intervals throughout the flight. Jeremy, although only seven years old, liked the role of 'big brother' but Pat thought that he was sometimes a bit unkind to Sam. Simon would laugh at her concerns and said that he had been exactly the same with his younger sister. Throughout the flight Sam insisted that Jeremy came with him when he went to the toilet and his worry about flying made him need to use the toilet at frequent intervals. Jeremy himself felt a little worried about using the toilet in case he got stuck in there, but he did not like to show his worry because he was the 'big boy'. Pat offered to go with Sam but he indignantly refused her offer. Simon was busy reading and did not even notice that Sam had been to the toilet at least five times in the past half hour.

In this example, Sam felt protected by his older brother who was pleased to take on the 'big brother' role. Remember that toddlers and young children can worry about vomiting, urinating and eating in the strange environment of the plane. They can also worry about being in the presence of so many strangers, having to wear seat belts and not being able to move about the cabin freely. Older siblings are often best placed to 'look after' younger siblings provided that they are willing to do so and are themselves not too anxious.

Couple problems and flying with children

The stress of travel can exacerbate any problems within a couple (see *Chapter 6*) and these, in turn, can affect the children. Although parents may try very hard to hide their difficulties from their children, it is not always possible to do so, and the older the child the more he or she will pick up the parents' problems. Children may sense tension between their parents; feel that mum worries excessively about flying; or that dad becomes very short-tempered with all the children just before a flight. Sometimes a child's difficult behaviour in the airport and the cabin may be a reflection of parental problems.

Case study

Beth and Ed had two children aged four and two. They were Americans living in the UK who flew home frequently in order to give their children a sense of their origins and to visit grandparents. Beth and Ed had just started to have marital counselling because of their bitter and unresolved quarrels. At the airport Beth and Ed were furious with each other and each parent dragged a reluctant child by the hand. Beth was saying through clenched teeth to her two-year-old, 'Come on honey, you will be able to see the clouds'. Meanwhile, the four-year-old pulled at his father's hand and wanted to go into every shop in the airport, having a tantrum and screaming if his father would not go with him. He also kept blowing loudly on the whistle his father had given him in case he got lost in the airport. Once on the plane, with increasing tension between their parents, the two children ran riot and were uncontrollable. They would not settle even with the toys given out by the cabin crew. They finally dropped exhausted in the newly vacated seats nearby. Beth and Ed maintained a frosty silence, each feeling that the other was to blame for the children's behaviour.

This scene illustrates the nightmare dreaded by all parents travelling with their young children. The following strategies may help:

- try to separate couple problems from parenting issues
- focus on your children's needs

- ask other experienced travellers for tips on flying with children
- do not try to resolve couple problems while preparing to fly with your children but put them temporarily on the 'back burner', at least for the flight's duration
- try to agree on 'rules' and 'roles' about the children long before the flight
- prepare your children for the flight by telling them what to expect.

Significant life-events

Significant events in the family, seemingly unconnected with the flight, may unsettle a child who, in turn, displays more obvious signs of in-flight turmoil. Events such as a recent death of a grandparent, bullying at school or parental divorce may make for a more uncomfortable flight emotionally if the children are upset by these events. Journeys from or to dying or sick relatives can be especially upsetting for young children, particularly if they are not told all the details and do not fully understand what is happening. Children can be upset by their parents' distress especially if they have no explanation for this.

Having described some of the relationship issues and underlying psychology which can affect children, the rest of this chapter will discuss common problems encountered by children and their parents before and during a flight.

Pre-flight preparation panics

Preparing well in advance for your family's needs can greatly reduce last minute panics. It is safer to assume that you will have to provide all the necessary food, equipment and toys than to rely on the airline, as services for children vary enormously between airlines. Make 'to do' lists that are achievable and practical and involve your children. Children enjoy being involved and part of the excitement of a holiday lies in the fun of preparation. Give each child their own small bag to pack with in-flight toys and books and their favourite walkman tapes. You may need to provide some supervision depending on their ages. Throughout your journey, remember to:

- ask what services are available for your baby or child?
- be clear about your requirements; for example, a baby's carrycot on the flight.

Parents' anxiety and exhaustion on the plane

Whenever possible, share the burden of flying with children with your partner. Try to discuss in advance who will do what with whom at the airport and on the flight. For example, before a long flight, discuss which parent will be 'on duty' for which child and for how long. At least each of you will then have some opportunity to have some rest. Discuss your concerns together, as they can assume huge proportions when they remain locked in your head.

Case study

Bob and Gina had three children aged four, two and a half and three months. They were flying to Australia to see Gina's parents and to join the family in celebrating her younger brother's wedding. The four-year-old, Judy, was very excited at the prospect of being a bridesmaid and she and her brother, Dave, kept asking Bob and Gina all kinds of questions about Australia and flying. Being a methodical person, Gina had planned everything meticulously. Her main worries focused on her fear of exhaustion and coping with the baby, Jo, on the flight; it was their first flight with their three children and it was a long flight. She knew that Bob was being hassled at work, so she kept her worries to herself — after all, they were going on this long trek to visit her family. But, on the evening before the flight, it finally proved too much for Gina and she became tearful and said to Bob that she just could not cope. He had thought that such a long flight might prove beyond Gina's coping abilities but she was so set on going, and the older two children seemed so excited, that he did not voice his reservations. Once Gina had shared her worries with Bob, she felt enormously relieved. They discussed their plans again and Bob was able to reassure Gina that he would take charge of Judy and Dave, and suggested that when Jo went to sleep, she should also try to sleep. They made additional plans on how to keep Judy and Dave amused, by buying new puppets which they had seen recently on the television.

Children's anxieties about travel

Depending on their age, children can worry about various different aspects of flying. Their age and maturity will also determine whether they are able to tell you about them. Their worries range from: falling out of the sky, a fear of heights, becoming separated from parents, being air sick, experiencing pain in the ears, getting stuck in the plane toilet, not understanding the strange noises in the plane, having to be strapped into the seat, encountering strangers and eating unfamiliar food.

Prepare children both practically and emotionally for a flight, especially if it is their first flight. With very young children this is more easily done with pictures of planes and aircraft cabins, as well as pictures of the destination to which they are travelling. Tell them what to expect and how they might feel. Try to spend a calm day before travelling and set out for the airport in good time. Preparation in advance will reduce last minute frenetic activity. Compiling and using check lists will help. A quiet look round the airport lounge, with explanations of what they are looking at, will help to reduce a child's anxieties. Some airports have separate rooms for feeding and changing babies and a few airports now offer play areas for older children, but these facilities vary considerably. Try to find a quiet, secluded corner of the lounge for you and your children. Staying put and staying calm helps everyone and a quiet corner will reduce the chances of children getting lost. Do not forget to take the all-important cuddly toy or teddy or blanket.

If your child seems excessively upset or difficult on a flight:

- ask yourself what else may be bothering your child
- it is not usually useful to ask your child 'why' they are behaving in a particular way or what else is troubling him or her. Observe their behaviour and mood as a way of trying to provide some answers to their 'difficult' behaviour

- some calming, diversionary tactics may be all that are needed to fly in greater comfort, such as telling a story, playing 'I spy' or having a snack
- a dose of humour can help child and parent. If too stressed yourself to be funny, arm yourself beforehand with a children's joke book.

Children getting lost

Airports and planes can elicit archetypal responses from all of us. The strangeness of the environment can sometimes cause fears more appropriate to coping in the jungle, and some children and parents fear getting lost in the confusing and strange setting of the airport. Most large air terminals have a meeting point and public announcement system and enquiry desks which older children can use. Tell your children, before arrival at the airport, what to do if they are separated from you. In addition, attach a label with their name and flight details to smaller children who might wander. A whistle attached to a child, with strict instructions on its use, can also help locate a lost child.

Seating

Thinking through the seating requirements for you and your children can reduce the stress induced by flying with the family.

Babies: Airlines sometimes seat families with babies in the first row of seats facing the bulkhead and long-distance flights often provide carrycots. On most airlines the carrycot is only big and safe enough for a baby up to 10 kg. Take your baby's favourite blanket as it can be very comforting.

Toddlers: Experienced travellers with small children, on a long flight, usually recommend taking seats in the middle section between the two aisles (when there is a middle section). Often there are more seats in this row than between the window and aisle with a greater chance of a vacant seat. Furthermore, the armrests usually lift so that a small child can spread across their seat and a parent's knee and, hopefully, sleep. You might want a row of seats near a toilet. Ask for extra pillows and blankets as soon as you board in order to make younger children more comfortable and to prepare them for sleep. Creating a sense of a 'base', using blankets, can also help anxious children to settle down.

Older children: They will usually settle down wherever they are seated. Many will enjoy the opportunity to look out of the window and try using the various gadgets. Try to relax yourself and keep an eye on your children, but do not stress yourself or them by being overvigilant.

Even though cabin crew are usually helpful to families flying with children, it sometimes pays to look around to see if you can spot any better placed seats; for example, a row with an extra empty seat. Older siblings often enjoy the sense of being 'grown-up' if they sit together a few rows away from parents.

Taking off and landing

Physical discomfort

It is more difficult for your ears to adjust to the pressure change when the plane is descending than when it is taking off, and young children appear to be more sensitive to these air pressure changes than older children or adults. For small babies the two manoeuvres that will ease the pain are crying and swallowing. Therefore, giving the baby a drink on taking off and landing, if crying distresses you, will do the trick. However, there is not much that you can do about a baby crying, so it is probably best just to grin and bear it. For older children and adults, swallowing, chewing or yawning can also help; chewing gum or sucking a sweet will encourage swallowing. However, a consistently successful method of popping your ears is to use the valsalver manoeuvre — in this technique, you pinch your nose, close your mouth and blow against your cheeks keeping your mouth closed. You gradually increase the pressure of your blow until your ears pop. Repeat the technique if you only succeed with one ear. (This will not work and should not be tried if you have a cold with a blocked nose.)

Psychological discomfort

For some children, as well as adults, the most anxiety-provoking times of the flight are taking off and landing. *Chapter 3* refers to overcoming fears associated with flying with specific strategies in this area. However worried an adult may be about take-off and landing, you should remember that young children, particularly on their first flight, do not know what to expect.

Explain to them what will happen and what they are likely to experience in words that they can understand. It helps to normalise the experience for children, especially if they are worried. For example, you could link the initial butterfly sensation in their stomachs with similar feelings to the first occasion they jumped into a swimming pool. The younger the child, the less s/he can understand about take-off procedures. They may, for example, become alarmed at the appearance of sudden pain in their ears but a calm explanation as well instructions on what to do, will relieve any anxiety as well as any pain.

Food and drink

Although some airlines will provide children's meals if ordered in advance, and will serve them when the children are hungry, most airline catering is geared to the needs of adults. The golden rule to avoid both your stress, and hungry babies and children, is to take all necessary supplies plus a bit extra with you. Be prepared for:

- baby's and toddler's needs: take food in small jars, extra plastic spoons, paper plates, paper bibs, small bottles of drinks (even if you are breast feeding)
- older children's needs: lots of snacks (preferably not too messy) and drinks.

Be tolerant of:

- mess: take a change of clothes and underwear for the children
- fuss: children may respond to either the excitement

or the anxiety of flying by making a fuss about the food, seating, noise, their siblings

- unhealthy food and drinks: your children's teeth will probably survive the effects of sweets and sweet drinks and you might survive the journey better by 'giving' in to demands for them. It makes sense to avoid carbonated drinks as far as possible, as they can cause some abdominal discomfort through their 'bloating' effect
- noise: babies cannot help crying and it helps with ear pain when taking off and landing. Just concentrate on your child's needs and forget about the other passengers
- reactions to your child: ignore the disapproving ones, ignore your own embarrassment and welcome any approving comments from other passengers.

Boredom

As with adults, children sometimes find long flights boring. The feelings of boredom can make any cabin discomfort feel worse and vice versa; long stretches of boredom can make the discomfort in the cabin feel awful. In order to break the vicious circle:

- take enough toys, books, walkman plus tapes and games with you and give them out gradually throughout the flight. Do not rely on the give-away toy bag handed out to children by some airlines; they may not suit your child's needs: being too childish or too grown-up for them

- ensure as much comfort as possible using the strategies mentioned above and by getting the best seating, enough blankets, sufficient drinks.
- play games with the children, such as 'I spy', guessing games, puppet games
- keep to a small child's normal routine, as far as possible, so that sleep times are the same as at home. On a long flight it may help to get into the routine of the place and time of your destination.

Motion sickness

Turbulence can be troublesome to those unused to air travel as well as to those who are anxious fliers and motion sickness may sometimes occur without any turbulence. If you or your children are subject to motion sickness, try one or some of the following:

- take motion sickness tablets before take-off, your doctor can advise you on the most suitable preparation for you and your child. Some travel sick tablets cause drowsiness which may be an advantage on a long flight
- ginger capsules, available from health food shops, are an old-fashioned remedy which some people find effective. Check with the health shop that the capsules are appropriate for your child's age and weight
- special wrist bands with a pressure ball sewn in, which presses on an acupuncture point on the wrist, can be useful and are available from many travel

accessory shops as well as many airports. There are instructions with these wrist bands recommending where to place them

- ask your child to close his or her eyes. This avoids the conflicting signals between his or her eyes and the inner ear (which detects changes in movement) and thus reduces the nausea
- encourage your child to lie down. Older children can try to recline their seats, put a pillow behind their shoulders and tilt their head backwards so that it is nearly horizontal. The less vertical movements affecting the inner ear the better
- cool the face as much as possible either by increasing the air flow through the overhead air jets or by bathing the face with a cold damp flannel
- avoid giving aspirin to your child as one of its effects is disturbing the inner ear
- even though it may appear paradoxical, it is often helpful to hold an air sickness bag near to the mouth of a nauseated child (or adult, for that matter). Children do worry about where they will be sick. Having the bag nearby reduces the anxiety and that, in itself, can reduce the feelings of nausea.

Sick children

Most of us who have flown with young children have faced the dilemma of what to do about a sick child. It is usually obvious which course of action to follow if the child is very ill just prior to a holiday flight but the decision is more difficult if the child does not seem to be that ill, or the reason for the journey has deep emotional significance, such as visiting a dying grandparent. It is worth remembering that seemingly trivial colds or earache can cause great pain, particularly on taking off and landing. The dry atmosphere of the aircraft also seems to affect small children adversely, especially those just recovering from, or just brewing, a cold or respiratory infection. Just splashing faces with water or spraying water onto the face can increase the comfort level although a visit to your General Practitioner before your trip may be advisable. Taking out adequate travel insurance is also advisable — but do read the small print first.

Sleeping on a flight

Most children will eventually fall asleep on a long flight. By the time that they do fall asleep you may be exhausted. If your children are asleep and you are tired, do not delay, just get as comfortable as possible and try to get some sleep yourself. Most strategies for trying to get to sleep in a plane are concerned with finding and making your seat as comfortable as possible, as described under the heading *Seating*.

The lists given above are by no means complete but they will spark off your own ideas about flying with children. Most of all, they are to be used to enable you to enjoy travelling with your children.

8

Understanding passenger behaviour

There is something about air travel that seems to affect some people's behaviour. The quiet, reclusive person is prompted to become angry and demanding; the aggressive salesperson displays anxiety and appears withdrawn and the happily married wife or husband travelling alone becomes a predator and would appear to have only sex on his or her mind. Of course, these are inaccurate stereotypes, but they nonetheless convey how unique situations can affect how we think and what we do. Unfortunately, the risk of harm to ourselves increases if we are exposed to new situations and our usual methods of coping are untested or inadequate. This chapter addresses how our behaviour is affected by travel and highlights some ideas as to what we can do to make our journey safer and more comfortable.

Safety is of primary concern to the airline industry as well as to passengers. For decades, engineers, pilots, air traffic controllers, psychologists and others have continually sought to make air travel safer by improving the skills of pilots, designing safer aircraft, properly maintaining aircraft, developing more accurate methods for predicting weather, and by improving communications between pilots and air crew and air traffic controllers. Most research has focused on the performance of crew and airline personnel. It is only in the past five years that there has been a concerted effort to learn more about passenger behaviour and the experience of air travellers. This is in part due to an interest in how passengers behave in emergency situations, as well as the advent of in-flight violence, or 'air rage', both of which are addressed in this chapter.

The aircraft cabin and stress

Research has demonstrated that the unique environment of the aircraft cabin directly affects behaviour. The air inside an aircraft cabin is usually dry and low in humidity – even drier than the Sahara Desert. Dry air and low cabin pressure have been found to produce stress, irritability and also reduce our ability to make sound judgements. It may help to explain why you may have a headache, are a bit short-tempered and feel irritable. Noise levels from the engines and outside air rushing past the aircraft are an additional source of stress. Loud noise also results in people having to raise their voices which can be misconstrued as aggressive behaviour, thereby increasing tension between people.

Cramped conditions on board aircraft may also make people feel more stressed. Passengers seeking to claim their territory are known to have acted aggressively towards fellow passengers and crew, and most people who have flown will have encountered the overhead locker bully. This is the person who aggressively fills the whole locker with his/her belongings and pushes you and your belongings out of the way. He/she is probably also the same person who reaches the seat before you do, claims both armrests and snatches the last copy of the newspaper. Psychologists have found that emotional reactions intensify and stress increases when strangers invade personal space. This may be aggravated when we share space with a wide range of strangers of varying cultures, ethnic backgrounds, and differing ages.

Unruly passenger behaviour

Airline passengers may also be more emotionally aroused which can intensify how they cope with stressful or unfamiliar situations. They may be; anxious about separating from a loved one, homesick, concerned about a business trip, upset that they cannot console a distressed child, lonely, excited, or even worried that their spouse will discover that they had been having an affair while abroad. For potentially aggressive passengers, being away from familiar surroundings may lead them to believe that it is acceptable to act differently and that rules which govern behaviour on the ground do not apply at 35000 feet in the sky flying over the ocean.

A further factor to consider is the excessive use of alcohol among some passengers. This may be partly because it is freely available and partly to offset boredom or to cope with a fear of flying. If you add to this: restlessness from excessive 'seat belts on' conditions; longer non-stop flights in more cramped aircraft; sleep disturbance, especially on east-west flights; the effects of certain prescribed or illicit drugs; delays; claustrophobia and even indifferent or aggressive cabin crew, then you have a lethal combination. While we would never condone violence on board aircraft, it now becomes possible to understand how some acts of so-called air rage develop.

Case study

Bill is an overweight telecommunications manager on his way to an important meeting in the USA. He is tired, cross and angry. He had to stay awake the previous night to put the finishing touches to his business presentation and the contract affects his job security. As his company is cutting back on travel expenses, he finds himself booked in economy class but he hates cramped seating. Fortunately, however, there is a vacant seat between his window seat and the occupied aisle seat, so he puts a pile of his papers and some of his hand luggage on the seat, leaving no space for his neighbour. Bill ignores this man's polite request for some part of the middle seat. He orders some drinks from the flight attendant to help to relax and unwind. By the time that the meal is served, Bill is almost faint with hunger, but also becoming a little clumsy as he has his third whiskey. He stretches across his neighbour to take another roll from the flight attendant and accidentally knocks the cup of coffee out of his hand. His neighbour, who has so far ignored Bill's inconsiderate behaviour, feels that he has been provoked beyond endurance. He stares at Bill and then tells him what he thinks of him. Bill retaliates by trying to punch him.

Recent media attention has focused attention on the increasing frequency and severity of acts of violent in-flight behaviour by passengers which is usually directed at cabin crew. 'Air rage', as it is commonly termed, is of special concern to those in the airline industry as well as to many passengers because of the all too frightening consequences of serious injury to the crew and to fellow passengers.

It is difficult to obtain accurate statistics of the number of air rage incidents because some airlines claim that they have not kept accurate records over the years. Also, there is no accepted definition of 'air rage'. One airline might consider drunkenness as a problem while, for another, it could be violence or verbal threats. In spite of these difficulties, limited data has recently been made available. Of the world's largest international carriers, all have reported an increase in the number of such incidents and, more alarmingly, more serious cases.

Cabin crew interactions with passengers appear to be the

single greatest trigger of disruptive behaviour. This usually occurs in response to a request for a passenger to behave in a particular way; for example, to return to their seat, extinguish a cigarette, remove headphones or put a seat in an upright position. Some passengers react angrily because they resent being told what to do, do not feel in control of their situation or may not understand the reason for the request or command.

We know from newspaper headlines that many air rage incidents have been triggered by drunk passengers, but the over use of alcohol by no means accounts for all cases. However, violence may come at the end of a long sequence of related issues, such as stress, feeling upset or angry, cramped conditions, a demanding personality, and so on. Some recent examples of incidents include:

- when denied another drink, an intoxicated first class passenger (dubbed 'patient zero' by those who study so-called 'cabin fever') proceeded to pull down his pants and underwear and defecated on the cabin floor and food trolley
- on a flight out of Los Angeles, a passenger struck a flight attendant because he was told that there were no more chicken meals for dinner
- a disgruntled passenger on another flight tried to throw a flight attendant out of an emergency exit
- when asked to remove his headset while the aircraft was taxiing, a passenger struck a flight attendant so hard that he was sent flying into the next row of seats
- a male passenger, later found to be under the influence of LSD, started preaching to and blessing other passengers. He also wanted to enter the flight

deck in order to bless the cockpit crew. It needed four people to restrain him, but not before a flight attendant was severely injured

- after being denied an upgrade to first class, a passenger and his travelling companion threatened to 'take the plane down'. During the ensuing fracas to restrain the passenger, a flight attendant received second degree burns after being scalded by coffee

- a passenger seriously injured a flight attendant by hitting her with a bottle of duty free alcohol . She had to have over 30 stitches.

Contrary to some popular wisdom, in-flight violence is not confined to economy class passengers who, it is assumed, may be reacting against crowded and cramped conditions. Anecdotal evidence suggests that business class passengers and those who are members of frequent flier programmes, can be especially demanding and aggressive as they have higher expectations of service.

How have the airlines responded to the threat of violence on board aircraft? Some airlines have recently taken steps to combat in-flight violence. British Airways, for example, now display warning cards to unruly passengers as well as teaching cabin crew how to physically restrain them if required. Courts passing down custodial sentences to offenders conveys the message that in-flight violence is socially unacceptable. However, for any deterrent to be really effective, a would-be perpetrator must believe that there is a significant chance that they will be caught and that the consequences will be severe. This requires consistency in approach throughout the airline industry. Equally, every incident, however minor, must not go unpunished.

Airlines do not easily admit to complicity in this problem, yet it transpires that some incidents have been the result of a lethal combination — a disgruntled passenger, treated poorly at check-in, who becomes inebriated on the flight, and is served by an over-worked or jet-lagged cabin crew member. A seemingly minor trigger event (eg. an unanticipated delay or non-availability of a special meal) has lead to verbal or physical violence. These acts, however, are probably more than an impulsive venting of fury. They may signal a worrying breakdown in the relationship between passengers and flight crew. Flight attendants may experience role confusion. Their principal role, according to the airlines, is to ensure cabin and passenger safety, yet the expectations of passengers are quite different. Cabin crew report that if lack of attention to safety demonstrations is a reliable measure, passengers are more interested in being pampered by cabin crew than in the important matter of safety. Passenger apathy about air rage is an added problem. All passengers should be reminded, however, that any assault on a fellow passenger or member of the cabin crew also puts them at risk. Responsibility toward the safe and efficient operation of the aircraft is a shared one.

Redesigning aircraft cabins so that the size of seats and the space between them is increased as well as improving environmental conditions, by increasing humidity and air pressure, seems obvious, but is unlikely to prove a popular solution for airlines because of the revenue implications. However, there are other factors that may be more amenable to change. Crew selection and training needs to take into account skills for coping with threatening situations. The role of ground staff in denying boarding to unruly or intoxicated passengers needs to be acknowledged and strengthened. Turning a blind eye on the ground merely shifts the problem to the cabin environment where the consequences may be far more serious. After all, the reality in aviation is that you cannot simply 'pull over' to the hard shoulder and throw an unruly passenger off a flight. Promoting a safety conscious image, rather than one that emphasises seat-side service to passengers can reduce the confusion that may exist about the role of cabin crew. Whatever your grievance, keep your temper out of the aircraft cabin or, at least, in check otherwise your next trip may be to a court and then to prison.

What if you encounter a noisy or disruptive neighbour? Stay calm. Avoid direct confrontation with the fellow passenger as this may make the situation worse. Discretely alert the cabin crew, but do so away from your seat where that passenger may overhear you. At least one member of crew is likely to be in the galley area. Most crew members are trained to deal with violent or threatening passengers and will not hesitate to inform the Captain and summon the help of colleagues or other passengers if there is any threat of danger. You can also ask to be moved to another seat if there is available space. Do not be reticent about reporting a situation that concerns you; it may make it more difficult to manage later on and the consequences may be more serious. Remember that the law is on your side.

Avoid becoming a disruptive passenger by learning how to; relax, to cope without smoking, drink alcohol in moderation, and to cope with your fear of flying. Test the effect of a mild tranquilliser to help you deal more effectively with any grievances several days before flying.

Flight crew behaviour

Although not the main focus of this chapter, readers may be interested to know something about the experiences of flight crew and how they cope with the stress of their job and air travel. This understanding will hopefully help the reader to appreciate the problems that crew face and the multiple demands on their physical and psychological resources. In the first instance, it must be remembered that crew share the same environment as passengers. They are exposed to most of the same conditions within it, such as cramped working spaces, decreased oxygen levels, low humidity, noise and they also suffer jet lag on some flights. Cabin crew work in this environment and pushing trolleys, preparing food, lifting hand luggage and attending to the safety of the flight is all the more exhausting given these conditions. The one major exception is that there is usually an improved supply of oxygen on the flight deck, in order to prevent the pilots nodding off for a nap or feeling sluggish due to the undersupply of oxygen.

Most flight crew are required to undergo frequent and vigorous testing of their proficiency at a number of tasks, and are also subjected to medical tests, sometimes as often as every six months. Flying an aircraft is physically demanding and also leads to emotional stress. Sleep may be impaired due to the length or destination of a flight, which in turn may affect work performance and mood. Demands from passengers may be incessant; a breakdown in the in-flight entertainment system, attending a passenger who is unwell, or caring for unaccompanied children or a fearful flier add to the stress and demand of the job. It is not surprising that all crew have to be fit, agile and tolerant.

Crew also have to endure separation from their family, and their social life 'back home' may be impaired due to their rostering and the requirements of the job. Work in any public service industry is inevitably stressful and, additionally, cabin crew sometimes have to contend with demanding or insolent passengers. Shift work can be disruptive as it is sometimes unpredictable and may not coincide with the routines of family and friends, thereby removing these relationships as a potential buffer against job stress. Although the public perception is of a well-knit crew team, it is often the case that crew on large airlines may not have previously worked together. It may be a constant challenge and source of stress to establish new work and social relationships with colleagues, and last minute crew changes reinforces the feeling of impermanence in these relationships. These observations may help the reader to understand why it requires a particular combination of physical and psychological skills to work as flight or cabin crew.

Passenger behaviour in emergencies

Contrary to some popular wisdom, the overwhelming majority of aircraft accidents are survivable. Nowadays, modern aircraft are built with safety and surviving in mind. No aircraft can be licensed to carry passengers unless stringent safety criteria have been carried out. Some of these tests are repeated when engineers service aircraft on the ground, while others are routinely carried out before each flight.

For the average passenger, the main exposure to the 'safety loop' is the safety demonstration before the flight or a delay due to a technical problem. The safety briefing is designed to familiarise passengers with some of the safety equipment available and procedures to be followed in the event of an emergency but do not involve passengers in trying them out for themselves. This is understandable, as no flight would ever get away on time if each passenger had to demonstrate how he or she would don a life jacket, open a cabin door or adopt the 'brace' position. However, going through the procedure in your mind is a good alternative. The simple fact is that those who are prepared stand a better chance of surviving an accident. The stress of an emergency situation, as well as the environmental conditions that may prevail (eg. smoke or debris), are far removed from the 'news delivery' calmness depicted in the safety demonstration. Remember that the cabin crew are there primarily to ensure safety and you should not hesitate to ask questions if you wish. Some hints that can improve your confidence and chances of surviving an emergency include:

- take the safety demonstration seriously. No matter how often you fly, your attention to the demonstration reinforces what you know and, also, aircraft differ in their layout and design
- read the safety information card; in your mind, rehearse the procedures
- remember to put on your own oxygen mask first before helping others; without oxygen, you will not be much help to others
- count the number of rows between your seat and the nearest exit in front of and behind you; in a smoke-filled cabin, that could help you to know when you have reached an exit

- when people are in shock they sometimes behave in an uncharacteristic way. For example, they may refuse to leave the aircraft when ordered to evacuate. Follow instructions but also apply common sense.

Remember that the crew will do all they can to ensure your (and their) safety, but it is your responsibility to be informed and prepared. It could also save your life.

Risk-taking behaviour among travellers

Most of this book deals with air travel. This short section deviates slightly from this topic to consider some of the risks to the traveller in a foreign environment. Surveys of travel clinic attenders repeatedly confirm that travellers worry about becoming unwell while abroad, due to eating certain foods or drinking contaminated water. Some illnesses are entirely preventable and the health risks to the traveller can be significantly reduced by a visit to a travel clinic well ahead of the departure date and by following the advice given.

Research carried out among returning travellers, reveals that a proportion do not heed the advice given by experts and are unnecessarily exposed to infection, illness or other misfortune. This happens in spite of their knowledge and awareness of the risks. Three examples are:

1. Exposure to sexually transmitted diseases (eg. gonorrhoea, HIV) through unprotected intercourse with someone abroad.

2. Contracting malaria by not taking anti-malaria medication or not completing the full course of treatment.

3. Sunburn (and the increased risk of skin cancer) after inadequately protecting exposed skin.

Although these are different health problems, the common thread of 'risk-taking' among some travellers links them. There are several possible explanations why travellers might take unnecessary risks:

1. In terms of sexual risks, some people make judgements about the degree of risk to which they will be exposed according to the appearance of their partner(s). For example, healthcare professionals often hear from returning travellers statements such as, 'He looked too healthy to be infected'; or, 'She was young and good looking and didn't seem to be the type to be ill', or 'We only did it once to reduce the risk'. Of course, these beliefs are unreliable because sexual infections can be transmitted irrespective of the age or appearance of the person as a person may be infected but free of obvious symptoms.

2. When people are away from home and their usual routine, different decisions may be reached about the acceptability of certain risks. For example, someone may choose to have a one-night-stand while on a business trip because they believe that it poses no risk to the relationship with their partner. Similarly, having to take medication to prevent malaria is equated with ill health; this belief may conflict with the sense of fun and relaxation associated with recreation and being on holiday.

3. Travellers may argue that since they did not detect any mosquito bites on their body, they could not have been infected with malaria, thereby justifying their decision not to take anti-malaria pills. However, if a mosquito had bitten

them they would have not been able to prevent infection. In other contexts, we label this 'gambling behaviour' with its attendant risks.

Prevention of any of these health problems is associated with having to give up some fun or having to bring a measure of unwelcome intrusion into enjoyable situations. For example, where there is a sexual risk, it may necessitate the use of condoms or refraining from having intercourse. To prevent malaria, it requires taking pills (which may have an unpleasant taste), not only for the duration of the time the traveller is in a malaria-endemic area, but also before entering it and for some considerable period thereafter. And for the sun worshipper, the 'instant' tan (or burn) may have to become the gradual tan. Each of these situations is associated with some risk and the need to change certain ideas or behaviour. Ignoring the risks can prove dangerous or even fatal.

The best that a healthcare professional in a travel clinic can hope to achieve is to inform you of these and related risks, and the reasons for them, and encourage you to reduce the risks wherever possible through inoculations and behaviour change. Your intentions are a reasonable predictor of behaviour. For instance, young, single men travelling with friends are at greater risk of health problems for two reasons. Firstly, they may intend to take sexual and other risks while abroad. Secondly, the group may influence the individual and his intentions (for example, to tan responsibly or to take anti-malaria pills) may be swayed by what the group do (sleeping in the sun all day after getting drunk the night before).

Travellers frequently utter statements along the lines of, 'It won't happen to me; I'll be careful', or, 'I'll take the chance'.

While there is risk in many aspects of life, it seems reasonable to reduce this wherever possible. Travel increases the risk of health problems though many are entirely preventable. Ideas that may help to reduce your risk of becoming unwell while travelling include:

- be informed; visit a travel clinic or your doctor before you travel (and do not leave it to the last minute)
- do not ignore risks in the hope that they will disappear; the consequences may not be immediate, but they may be unpleasant or even life threatening
- consider as many risks as possible before you travel; decide how you will manage them and try to stick to your decisions
- risk may be increased when other factors are present (eg. alcohol or drug use) because the ability to make and keep to decisions may be impaired
- nusual or unpleasant symptoms of illness, even after your return; seek medical advice
- chant this mantra: 'It's better to have a good holiday and to stay well, than to have a brilliant time and return unwell'.

This book has considered how air travel affects us psychologically and physically. In order to reduce stress and cope with the demands of the situations, consider the following:

- Air travel might appear glamorous, but it is inevitably stressful. Anticipate a measure of stress, and lower your expectations of what will happen to reasonable proportions.
- Air travel is a service industry. There are bound to be some frustrations and disappointments and, wherever possible,

ignore them. Where you feel you have a legitimate complaint, tell a supervisor, but be reasonable. If necessary, put the complaint in writing, stating all the facts. Mention what you would consider reasonable compensation or what you feel would remedy the situation. Threatening language and tones rarely achieve anything.

- Arrive at the airport in good time. If possible, pre-book your preferred seat. Do not try to take on board too much hand luggage. You may be prevented from boarding with it.

- Insulate yourself against stress: bring plenty to read, a personal stereo, something to help you sleep, earplugs to shut out noise and learn to meditate.

- Avoid drinking too much alcohol. Not only will you feel dehydrated, but the effect is sometimes more potent due to the altitude and lack of humidity. Note the old adage; 'One in the air is worth two on the ground'.

- Remember that conditions in the aircraft cabin can make you feel irritable and uncomfortable. Apply moisturiser to counter the dryness; drink plenty of non-carbonated water to replenish the loss of body fluids in the dry cabin environment; move about the cabin from time to time to keep your blood circulation moving; wear loose, comfortable clothes; eat healthily.

- Listen to the safety demonstration. Read the safety information card. Rehearse procedures in your head.

- Take responsibility for your safety and health.

- Find time to enjoy your travel experience.

References

Aurelius M (1995) *Meditations* (abridged by R Waterfield). Penguin Books Ltd, London

Bowlby J (1975) *Attachment and Loss Vol 2, Separation.* Penguin Ltd, London

Ellis A, Gordon J, Neenan M, Palmer S (1998) *Stress Counseling: A Rational Emotive Behaviour Approach.* Springer Publishing Company, New York

Palmer S, Strickland L (1996) *Stress Management: A Quick Guide.* Folens Publishers, Dunstable

Palmer S (1999) The Negative Travel Beliefs Questionnaire (NTBQ). *The Rational Emotive Behaviour Therapist,* **7**(1): 48–51

Index

A

aggressive xii
air rage 116–118
air sickness 18
air terminal 55, 58–61, 107
air travel
    anxiety 87
    fear of xi
aircraft 116
airline meals 71
alcohol 117, 119
alcohol consumption
    relief of bordom, anxiety xiii
'all-or-nothing' thinking 6
amenities xii
anticipatory anxiety 18, 29–30,
    39, 42, 46
antidepressant medication 92
anxiety 15, 16, 19–20, 31, 36,
    39, 55, 89
apprehension 29
aromatherapy 71
attachment 99
attitude 1
    negative 8, 14
    realistic 8
    unhelpful8
avoidance 20

B

behaviour xi
belief 1, 4, 9
    negative 8, 14
    unhelpful 12, 18
    helpful 8
    realistc 8
Benson relaxation 52
bodily functions xi
body clock 70
    resynchronise 71
boredom 111
Bowlby, John 98

C

cabin crew xiii
cabin pressure 116
catastrophic imagery 45
catastrophic thinking 20, 22
Centre for Stress Management,
    London 2
children 97–114
children's anxieties about travel
    105–7
circadian desynchronisation 62
claustrophobia 19, 44, 88, 117
communication 81
communication difficulties xii

constructive emotions 12
coping imagery 45, 50
couple problems 101
crowds xii
culture 116

D

defence mechanism 20
delays xii, 18, 60
demands 2
denial of reality 5
depressive illness 91
drunk passengers 119

E

Economy class syndrome 73
emotional reasoning 31
emotionally aroused 117
emotions
    understanding xiv
expectations xi–xii, 1–2, 4
    management of xiii
exposure exercise 42

F

fear 15, 16, 17, 21
    irrational 29
    management of 23
fear of flying xiii, 15, 20
    causes of 18
Fear of Flying Survey (FFS)
    23, 39
feared situation 39

fidelity 75
flight attendants 121
flight crew behaviour 123
flying anxiety 16, 33
flying phobia 17, 33
flying phobics 45
flying-related anxieties 32
flying-related fears 32
flying-related phobias 32
flying with children 101

G

graded exposure 39

H

homesickness 117

I

in-flight violence 120
insecure attachment 99
Institute for the Psychology of
    Air Travel 23, 28, 30
intermittent spouse syndrome
    79, 80, 82
internal body clock 68
irritable xii

J

jet lag 62, 64–65, 67–69, 72
    coping with 67
    overcoming xiii
    symptoms 63

L

low self-esteem 20

M

massage 71
medication xiii
melatonin
    sleep hormone 70
memory impairment 58
mentally re-appraise 2
motion sickness 112

N

negative attitudes 2
negative beliefs 2, 7, 43
negative predictions 5
negative thinking 22, 29
negative thoughts 5, 44
negative travel beliefs questionnaire (NTBQ) 2, 42
noise xii
noise levels 70

O

obsessive negative thoughts 44
overgeneralising 6

P

panic attack 19, 20, 24, 31
parents
    over-protective 20
passenger apathy 121

passenger behaviour xiii, 115–130
    in emergencies 124
perfectionism 20
personal space
    invasion of 116
phobia xii, 15, 17
    irrational 29
    management of 23
phobic of flying 23
positive relaxation imagery 51, 52
problem-solving 9, 11
psychologically vulnerable xii
psychologists 17, 20, 23, 116
psychology 103
punctuality xii

Q

quality of service xii

R

relationships xi, 74
relaxation exercises 71
risk-taking behaviour 126

S

safety 115
seating 107
secure attachment figure 98
secure attachment 99
sedatives 39
self-defeating attitudes 12

self-defeating beliefs 12
self-talk 71
sensory impairment 58
separation 56, 98
shame 17
significant life-events 103
sleep xiii, 69, 70, 114
sleep cycles 68
sleep hormone
    melatonin 70
sleep patterns 69
sleeping difficulties 52
sleeping pills 70
stimulus 21
stress xi, xii, xiv, 1, 4, 14, 42,
    59, 60, 101
    different reactions xiii
stresses of flying xiii
stressful life events 19
stress-inducing beliefs xiii
stress-inducing thinking 12
stress-susceptible personality
    20
stretching exercises 73
symptoms of anxiety 86

T

task-focused 11
tensions 84
thinking styles xiii, 6
time projection imagery 51
time zones 63–64

travel
    associated stress 77
    effect on relationships 74
travel phobia 17
triggers of anxiety
    general 21
turbulence 18–19, 26, 30, 33,
    35, 51, 112

U

unconstructive thinking 11
unruly passenger behaviour 117
use of imagery 44

V

violent in-flight behaviour 118

W

worry 56